GREAT IMPRESSIONS

The Art and Technique of Rubber Stamping

by Patricia Garner Berlin

Flower Valley Press

Gaithersburg, MD

Acknowledgements

There have been so many influences in acquiring material for this book. Some sources were friends and teachers while others were total strangers with whom I struck up a conversation in a rubber stamp shop. Every artist has a personal touch and a unique way of presenting art but basically we all have the same goal in common, a love of personal markings on varied materials to enhance our daily lives.

The very first idea of writing this book belongs to Seymour Bress, after he admired a simple hand carved eraser stamped border on stationary I used for our correspondence. Helene Bress echoed his enthusiasm and both of them have been patient beyond measure amassing all the material sent to them in spurts by a fledgling writer.

A request for stamping art work appeared in a stamping magazine and several of the featured artists responded to the call for submissions. Word of mouth brought forth more artists and soon the project was represented coast to coast and finally, all the way to New Zealand. I owe a great debt of appreciation to all the artists for the use of their slides and actual work which was generously loaned to me. Dave Clem, an outstanding photographer, was patient and creative in arranging and photographing art work for a major portion of the book. A "How To" book would not be possible without the generous contributions of many craft manufacturers who sent samples of their products, all of which were used and evaluated. My friends, who were pressed into service as proof readers, were diligent and constructive with their opinions, and I thank them for all their work. Finally, I want to express my deep appreciation to my family for putting up with my everlasting demands for their input on carvings, text, and artwork.

- Pat Berlin

Editors: Peter Mitchell and Seymour Bress

ISBN: 1-886388-01-6

10 9 8 7 6 5 4 3 2 1

Printed and bound in Hong Kong

Contents

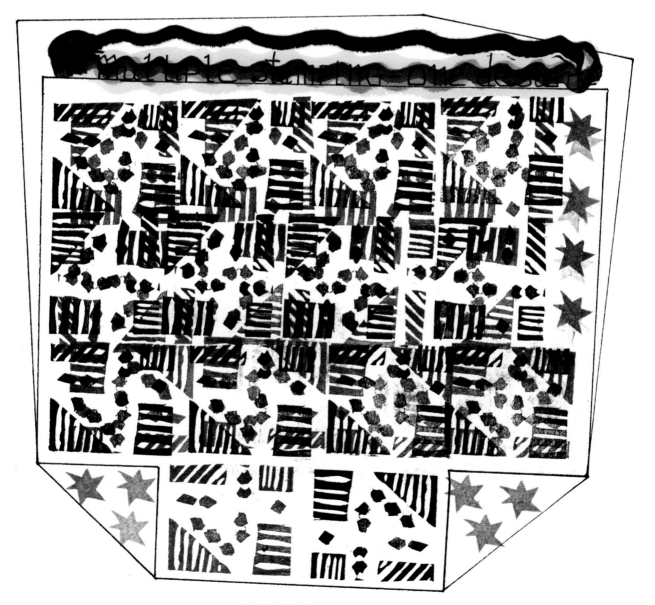

1. Variety of carved, stamped shapes by Pat Berlin.

Foreword

 arving and stamping is an easy, inexpensive and satisfying pastime that can be gratifying for beginners as well as for those more advanced. The rewards are immediate and results can range from the uncomplicated and lovely expressions of children and novices, to complex and deeply personal statements by serious fine artists. The possibilities are exciting and the fact that anyone can explore the pleasures of hand-carved stamps should have us all running out to buy erasers and get started.

Rubber stamping is not new, but it has only been in recent years that my enjoyment of stamps and stamping has been enhanced by my ability to make my own rubber stamps as part of the creative process. I am very appreciative for the advice given me by the author, who is an excellent teacher.

Learning a new technique is fun and offers the thrill of anticipation as the work reveals the artist's labor. Carving a rubber stamp is an easy way to have fun and be creative. The examples pictured in this book speak volumes about the opportunities for expression in this uncomplicated, yet eloquent, medium. For the beginner, stamping may open the door to a long-term, interesting hobby. In the hands of an experienced artist, stamping may produce astonishing results.

You may become seriously hooked on stamping, or you may discover a great hobby. In either case, your investment in time will not be wasted and the cost will come back to you in the form of gratification, as it always does when you work with your hands.

In what follows, Pat Berlin gives us a great introduction to hand-carved stamps and offers many applications with the same lightness and encouragement with which she teaches. Her rich background and years of experience will be evident to old friends and new readers alike.

Ruth Ann Petree
McLean, Virginia

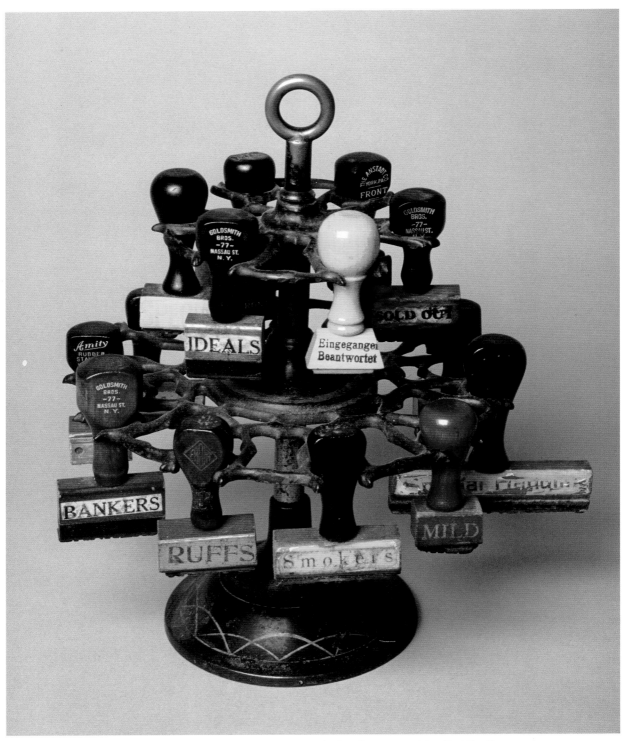

2. Collection of old stamps on antique metal holder. Collection owned by Pat Berlin.

Chapter 1:

Original Stamp Pad Art

 e live in a world of the ready-made. We buy stationery with our name on it. We buy greeting cards and gift wrap from a display in a store. Even our clothing is seldom one-of-a-kind. Flip through this book and what do you see? Fun, useful objects, and art, made from the simplest of tools - rubber stamps and some ink.

Stamp-pad art is within the reach of everyone. If you want something unique and completely your own, you can carve your own stamps. The materials needed are few and inexpensive. The process is simple and I will explain it to you, step-by-step. As you get into carving and stamping your own designs, your artistic life will become richer, more playful, and, most important, very personal.

But what if you do not want to carve your own stamps? There are thousands of excellent rubber stamps in the stores begging to be bought, brought home, and used. If you prefer to start your stamping with such stamps, let me show you how to use them in interesting and creative ways. The processes are uncomplicated and the results are almost immediate. You can combine just a few to many dozens of stamps in one project and rearrange them in endless combinations. Using manufactured stamps lets someone else be the artist for you. True creation will be in the way you use the stamps you have.

1

If you would like to carve your own stamps, but are not sure of your artistic ability, there is a vast range of copyright free art that is available to you. Books of such art and designs can be found in art supply shops and bookstores. You can have these designs made into rubber stamps for your personal use.

3. Sun Stamps by Paper Source.

Before you know it, you will be making stationery, greeting cards and postcards with your stamps. Wrapping paper and gift tags can be created for those special occasions and holidays. Clothing such as ties, T-shirts, aprons, scarves, and quilts, may be stamped. Labels, jigsaw puzzles, personal journals, handmade books, bookplates, bookmarks and jewelry may be added to the list. The range of possible stamped creations is almost endless.

4. Ivory Coast Alphabet Set.

Whether you carve your own stamps, or buy ready-made ones, there is much to explore. We will investigate stamp pads and inks for stamping. We will talk about color and the many sources available, from stamp-pad inks to color markers. We will look at some special techniques, such as masking. Also, there is embossing with colorful powders for a raised effect and a three-dimensional look. We will describe the many short cuts in producing one-of-a-kind items or production works of stamp art.

Your stamp art may be transient, or it may last forever. It's a satisfying way of expressing excitement or quiet thoughts while creating original designs. I urge you to give yourself the freedom to experiment or, as my first art teacher said, "Have the courage to make mistakes." It is from those "mistakes" that you learn the most. Whatever your talent and ability, you will be creating exciting art.

I encourage you to try several of the techniques presented in this book - and then to invent some of your own. Will your work end up in a museum? Perhaps, or perhaps not, but your artistic life will almost surely become enriched.

OK. Enough. Let's stamp.

5. Zodiac Stamp.

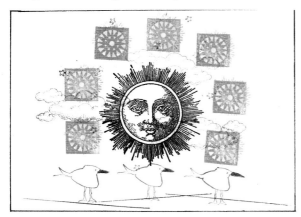

6. Create a scene from stamps.

7. Commercial stamps by Graven Images.

8. Capitol Inkers Anonymous Stamp Club stamp.

9. Capitol Inkers Anonymous Stamp Club stamp.

10. Stamps by Pat Berlin.

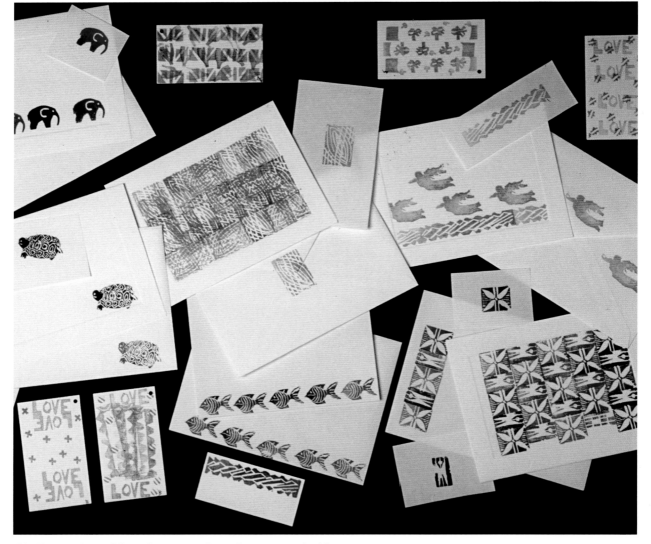

11. Examples of hand stamped stationery and gift tags.

Chapter Two

Stamp Pads and Ink

hen it comes to stamp pads and color, the range of choices is vast. Not only are basic colors available in stores, but designer colors such as celadon and sky blue are available, too. Also look for those rainbow pads, with stripes of assorted colors across them, as well as pads with metallic inks. When you enter a shop that carries a full line of ready-made stamps and stamping supplies, you'll be excited by the variety and want them all immediately. If you have just begun stamping, it might be best to invest in a few one-color pads. You'll see that, one by one, your stock of supplies will grow along with the number of your stamps, and eventually you may have them all. (See the "Resources" section for pads and supplies.)

Proper care of your stamp pads is important. A pad that is stored upside down keeps the ink on the surface where you want it. Make sure the lid is on tight so there is no leakage and the pad does not dry out. Re-inking a drying pad is done simply with refill ink applicators. When re-inking your pad, go over the entire pad, not just the center of it.

Continual stamping only in the middle of the pad will eventually depress the center and may cause uneven inking of your stamps. With an adequately inked pad, light stamping is all that is needed. There is no need to pound. Use all parts of the pad for your stamping.

To prevent muddying the color of your stamp pad, clean your inked stamp before using it for a second color. An uncleaned stamp will transfer some of its ink onto the new pad, changing its color. (See Chapter 4 for cleaning tips.) If you take care of your pads, they will serve you for years.

Some colors may well be worth mixing yourself. If you wish to mix your own, you'll need un-inked pads for those colors. Such pads can usually be found at stores selling office supplies or rubber stamps. Mix your colors first before applying them to an un-inked pad. A white dish, or clear glass bowl, makes the best container for mixing your inks, since the new color will have

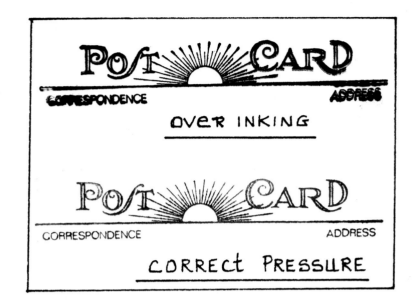

12. Stamp by Fruit Basket Upset.

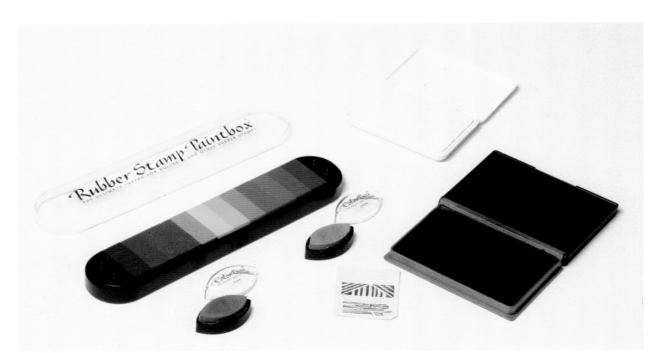

13. Examples of a few of the many brands of stamp pads now available.

the same look in the bowl as it will have when you stamp it on white paper.

There are some water based inks that give you a sharp, vivid, transparent stamped image and will stay wet longer in the pad. These inks are made for use on paper. If used on fabric, the print will wash out.

There are also washable fabric inks that come in a small bottle with a dropper attached. If you buy a brand that does not have a dropper, buy small, inexpensive eyedroppers at the drug store. (Never use the family eyedropper for your inks.)

When you need to ink or re-ink a pad, remember that over-inking may clog the fine lines on a stamp, resulting in a poor image. It is better to under-ink a pad than over-ink it since the imprints will be much sharper and defined. Apply inks slowly and evenly to the entire pad, and check frequently for sat-

14. Hand carved stamps by Pat Berlin.

15. Hand carved stamp by Pat Berlin.

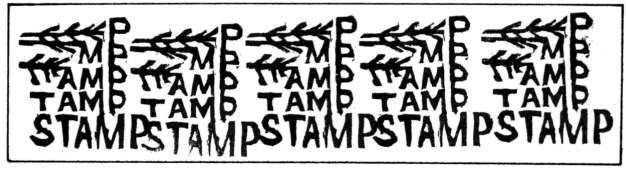

16. Hand carved word stamp by Pat Berlin.

uration by making sample stampings on scrap paper.

Multi-color stamp pads are marvelous to use and chances are you will want to get many of them in different combinations. My multi-color pads always start out looking fresh and vivid. Sometimes I get carried away with very arty images, though, and mess them up - giving me an excuse to buy more pads!

Here's how I work with multi-color pads. First, I mentally divide my pad in half horizontally, but actually use either the lengthwise bottom half or the top half for inking the stamp. The divided sections do eventually blend together, but that takes quite a long time to happen. I have not yet tossed out a "blended pad" because they produce interesting shades of color. If the stamp is larger than the pad, I do the inking in sections and use equal pressure so that the final design looks even in color tone.

On a small table I lay out scrap paper, rubber stamps, stamp pads, an old cloth or paper towel, and the final, good paper to be stamped. I press the stamp gently onto the multi-colored pad, lifting the stamp from one section to another covering several

17. Hand carved stamps by Pat Berlin.

18. Hand carved stamps by Pat Berlin.

19. Hand carved stamps by Pat Berlin.

sections, but I do not clean the stamp between inkings. When I press the stamp on the final paper, it produces a print that is multi-colored, with many flecks of color mixed together. This method results in a unique print, virtually impossible to duplicate. I stamp with an air of abandon, for a free, spontaneous look.

For some really different prints, start with a vivid solid color ink pad and ink your stamp. Leaving the ink on the stamp, gently press it on a black ink pad, and then print the image on your good paper. This method gives you an unusual black-over-color image that is interesting.

Take time to experiment and be sure to let all your stamped work dry thoroughly. When you use metallic inks, such as gold, silver or copper, you will find that they take longer to dry than other inks. For this reason, they are ideal to use when embossing, which is discussed in Chapter 9. Clean your stamps after using metallic inks so that you do not contaminate your other pads and don't let the inks dry and harden on your stamps.

20. Hand carved stamps by Pat Berlin.

21. Hand carved stamps by Jamie Brooks.

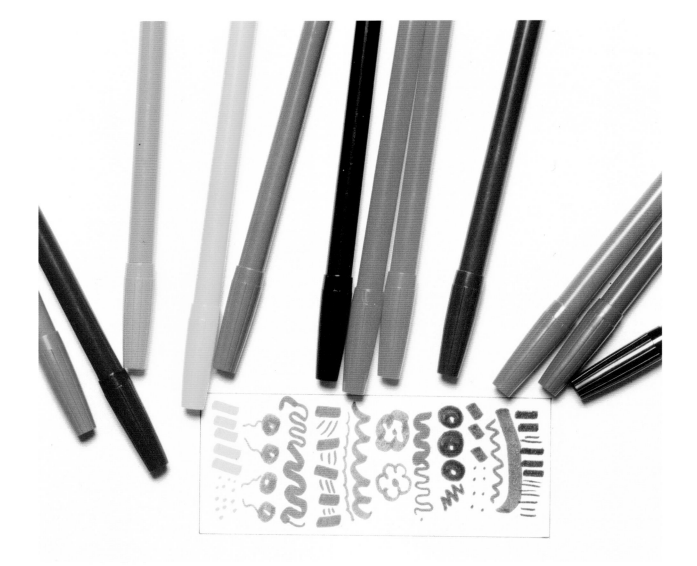

22. Use of markers - Marvy/Uchida markers.

Chapter Three

Using Color Markers with Stamps

dd pizzazz and subtle variations to your stamping with "felt -tip markers," "color markers," "marking pens," or whatever you call them. There are so many brands of markers available, and new products come out so frequently, that I will just mention the "dual-tipped" markers I enjoy using most. They have two working ends — one end is a brush-point, somewhat like a firm but flexible paint brush, and the other end has a firm, fine point. These markers are available in art supply stores and craft supply shops, but may be found in many toy shops and department stores as well.

Color markers can be applied directly to a stamp, or used in combination with a stamp that has already been inked on a pad. In the first method, for example, a stamp with a flower design may be colored using one color for the petals, another color for the center, a third for the stem, and yet a fourth color

23. Carved stamps by Pat Berlin.

11

for the leaves. Use either the brush end or the point end of the marker, depending upon the size and detail of the areas to be colored. Finally, press that stamp onto your paper. Your stamped image will have all the colors you applied to the stamp. For the clearest and most colorful print, you must re-apply the ink each time you want to stamp that same image. As marker inks can dry more quickly than stamp-pad ink, it is important to work quickly when using them. This method allows you to custom-color your stamping, to use several colors on one stamp, and not restrict the stamped design to the colors of your stamp pads.

Another marker technique combines two methods. First, using a solid-color stamp pad, stamp the design on a piece of paper. If the lines of the designs are cut away, there will be a white area depicting the design, separating it from the background area. Using the firm, pointed end of a dual-tip marker, fill in the white areas with another color. For example, print a butterfly, and color its wings with several colors.

Here's another coloring method. It requires some patience and care, but with it

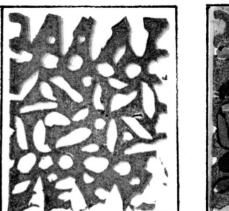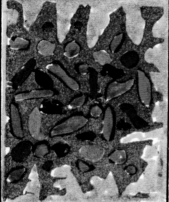

24. Hand carved stamps by Pat Berlin.

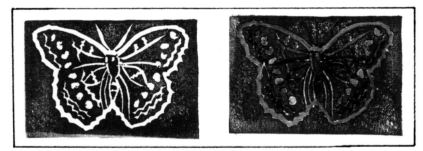

25. Hand carved stamps by Pat Berlin.

26. Hand carved stamps by Pat Berlin.

you may add a spot or two of color to a stamp that has already been inked on a stamp pad. First ink your image with the stamp-pad color you have chosen but don't stamp with it yet. Take a cotton swab — the kind with the little cotton "heads" on both ends of a stick — and moisten it sparingly with stamp cleaner, nail polish remover, or water. Carefully remove the stamp-pad ink from the areas where you would like to insert a new color. Now, with a dry swab, dry the cleaned-off areas to prepare them for the new color(s). Color those areas with your marker and stamp your design.

As with all your stamps, proper cleaning between color changes and after using your stamps is important in maintaining the "color health" of your stamps, pen tips and pads.

There is a type of marker that produces a unique effect when used on your stamped designs (Crayola® Overwriters®). The ink in these markers is designed to change color when the ink from one, the under color, touches the ink of the other, the over color. To see how they work, ink your stamp with a dark-color ink from your stamp pad and stamp it onto a piece of scrap paper.

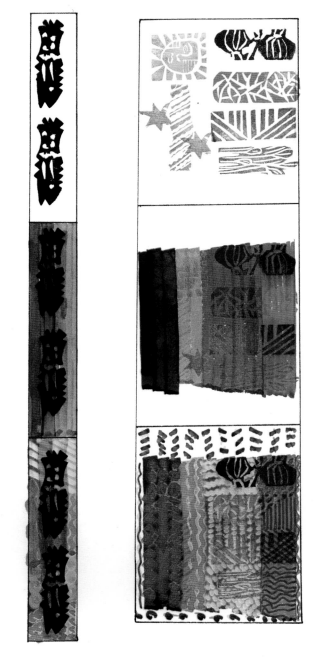

27. Hand carved stamps by Pat Berlin.

13

After the ink is dry, color the entire design with an "under-color" marker. You can use one color for a monochromatic effect, or several colors for a multi-color effect. Now the fun begins! With an "over-color" marker, make stripes, dots, wiggles, or whatever lines suit your fancy, over the previously colored design. The design is still visible through the veil of colors you've applied, but now it has a unique look. You can also color your paper first with the under color(s), then do the stamping, and finally apply the over colors.

Colored pencils should also be included in your repertoire. You may color an area of your paper with colored pencils before stamping on it, or, stamp an image first and then color within or around it. Some pencils have leads that are water soluble. With these pencils you can create the look of watercolor paint by stroking a damp brush over the penciled lines.

Decorative Chalks

Pastel chalks can also be used in conjunction with your stamps. These chalks work best on paper with a porous surface, such as bond papers, as opposed to those having a glossy surface.

28. By R. R. Brand.

29. Pressed chalks.

The chalks are wonderful to apply to paper as background color. Since no water is used, the paper stays flat and does not wrinkle. Apply the chalks with a cotton ball, a wad of tissue or a delicate touch of your finger. Stamp directly over the chalk. After the work is completed, apply an aerosol spray sealer to prevent the colors from smearing. A very light coat is all that is needed. If possible, do the spraying outdoors, but if you must do it indoors, do it in a room with adequate ventilation.

All your designs and techniques can be combined to make the final product your own unique creation. Dabble and enjoy yourself. Experimentation is the key to success with all of these methods, and curiosity helps generate new ideas.

30. Hand carved stamps by Pat Berlin.

31. By R. R. Brand.

32. Stamp pad journal by Pat Berlin.

Chapter Four

Cleaning, Storing and Mounting Your Stamps

f course, cleanliness is important when it comes to stamping and stamps should be cleaned between color changes and before storing them — but they will not be ruined if this advice is occasionally disregarded. To clean your stamps between color changes and before putting them away, place several layers of paper towels on a disposable plate and pour or spray glass cleaner onto the towels until the pile is saturated. It is best to use cleaners without ammonia, since ammonia dries out rubber. Stamp the inked stamps on these wet towels until the color no longer prints. Then, stamp them on dry paper towels or scrap paper for a final cleaning and to blot them dry. When the towels get very inky, simply turn the layers over and use the other side or replace them with new towels. If you feel you must soak your stamps to remove ink residues, do so in water that does not contain a cleaning agent.

For ink stains stubbornly adhering to your stamps, use a commercial rubber stamp cleaner (usually available with an applicator top), or a small amount of nail polish remover on a soft rag or cotton-tipped swab. Avoid scrubbing the stamp as this can tear the design, especially if it has fine lines. If you have a stamp that has a lot of fine lines which are clogged with ink, use a very soft, old toothbrush and put a little bit of nail polish remover, rubbing alcohol, or rubber stamp cleaner on it, and gently rub it over the stamp to remove the old ink and to bring the details back.

Metallic inks, such as gold, silver and copper, require a slightly different method of cleaning. For these inks, use a damp cloth which was slightly moistened with one of the cleaners mentioned above and simply clean the stamp by carefully rubbing off the remaining ink.

Some solvents are flammable. Use them with care, follow the manufacturer's cautions and be sure to dispose of your cleaning papers and rags appropriately!

Direct sunlight will cause your rubber stamps to dry and crack since the rubber hardens with exposure. If you store your stamps in a dry container and in a cool, dry place you will give them a longer life.

Where Is That Stamp?

As your collection of stamps grows, you will want to be able to find and identify your stamps quickly and easily. Dividing your stamps by subject is one way to keep your search for that certain stamp to a minimum. Labeling each stamp allows you to identify the stamp you want in a box crowded with stamps. Stamp your design on a self-stick label, wait for the ink to dry, then stick the label to the top of your stamp and trim it to size. If your stamp has a handle, place the label on the front of your stamp.

33. Stamps by Pat Berlin.

A Place For Every Stamp

Let us face one fact now - your collection of stamps <u>will</u> grow! As it does, storage and convenience become important considerations. So that your stamps will not have to be stacked one on top of another, store them in a shallow box. The box can be cardboard, plastic or wood, and should have a cover to keep out light and dust. Put a self stick label on each box to let you know what's inside.

A clear, plastic box with dividers, such as a parts box or fishing tackle box, allows you to see all your stamps at a glance. These boxes can usually be found in hardware stores, larger drug stores, and sporting goods stores. Also, many art supply stores carry art tool boxes which are similar to the parts and tackle boxes. These boxes can accommodate stamps, pads, inks, cleaners, and other necessities. When your collection gets very large, you can store your boxes of stamps and supplies in a tall bookcase that has narrowly spaced shelving, or in a music cabinet.

A blank sketch book can be converted to a handy reference book or log containing a stamped impression of all the stamps in your collection. It becomes your catalog of what you have, but can also have sections that serve as a repository for images of stamps you want to purchase or designs you want to carve in the future. For reference purposes, you can divide the book into categories, such as animals, people, objects, etc. Sketch books are always available in art supply stores. Also, blank books, which can serve the same purpose, are now every-where, from card stores to gift shops. The variety of their cov-ers and bindings is amazing and inviting, but if you want to design and decorate the cover of your blank book, choose one that has a blank cover which can be stamped. First design your cover on a piece of scrap paper that's the size of your book. Once you are satisfied with the design and know the steps you need to reproduce it, stamp the book cover. If you are hesitant about stamping directly onto the cover, stamp your design on a piece of good paper and then glue it to the book cover with a craft glue.

To Mount or Not To Mount

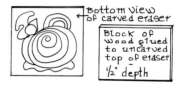

34. Pat Berlin.

Stamps that are mounted on a backing, with or without a han-dle, are usually preferred to the unmounted rubber stamps. I do not mount my stamps but prefer the direct, hands-on method of stamping. This method usually results in inky fin-gers, but fingers are easily cleaned with a wet rag or by wash-ing them with hand soap. Thin, latex medical gloves, which are found in most drug stores, can keep your fingers free from ink. Smudges or fingerprints on your finished creation are usually unacceptable, so bare-handed or gloved, take care.

Mounted stamps are the best alternative to inky fingers and easier stamping. There are many rubber stamp companies that offer unmounted stamps as well as mounted ones. The unmounted stamps are less costly and take up less storage space, but are not as easy to use as those stamps already mounted. If you want to mount the stamps yourself, check the advertisements in rubber stamp magazines for companies offering stamp mounts or make your own mounts from wood strips. A wooden base about 3/4" in height, and the same size as your stamp can be glued to the stamp with rubber cement. Other glues can be used, but rubber cement is recommended because it allows the stamp to be peeled off the mount and re-positioned, if necessary.

35. Hot Potatoes carving by Mary Benagh O'Neil.

Chapter Five

Carving Your Own Rubber Stamps

efore the advent of rubber and man-made materials, such as the plastics available today, stamping for decorative purposes was done with such easy-to-carve root vegetables as the potato and beet. Cork was also used to make simple designs. Small, carved wood blocks have long been used for stamping designs on fabrics. As materials improved, stamps increased in size and new methods of creating stamps came into being. Linoleum block carving is one example.

Today we have the option of using any of the above materials, but we also have a relatively new material to work with which is pleasant and easy to carve, long lasting and readily available - plastic erasers.

Materials and Tools

Let us look at some of the materials and tools you'll need for carving erasers. All of the items should be available at art-supply stores, but you may also find them in large office supply and stationery stores, arts and crafts stores and hobby shops, and in the craft sections of some department stores. There is a "Resources" section in the back of this book for more specific help.

Erasers

There is a great variety of erasers available today, but the best for carving are pliable and light in color. I use, and suggest you try, the white, plastic, semi-hard erasers since they are the easiest to carve. New products are always being developed, so do try different kinds. To test the suitability of the eraser for carving, bend it to see how much spring it has. If it feels very rigid, it will probably be too hard to carve and if it is too soft, it will crumble.

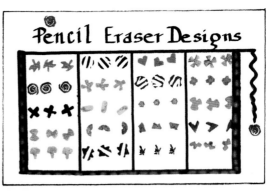

36. Pencil eraser designs.

The white erasers shown in photos 38 and 39 would be a good choice for carving. Also easy to carve are plastic novelty erasers, such as those with animal shapes. If you like the shapes they come in, you can use them as stamps with no further effort on your part.

Erasers at the end of pencils can be used "as is" or, small as they are, can be carved into even smaller shapes. The most common pencil-end eraser is 1/4" in diameter and the fatter, primary-school pencil eraser measures 3/8" in diameter. Before carving worn pencil erasers, trim them with a sharp knife so that the eraser is again flat on top.

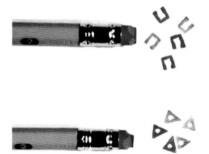

37. Pencil eraser stamps.

In addition to standard-size erasers, larger eraser "blocks" are now available. As with their smaller cousins, they are very easily carved. The entire block can be used for a large design or the block can be cut up into smaller sections.

Paper

And paper! The choices are so vast that we've devoted a whole chapter to it. For now, tracing paper is all you'll need for making and transferring designs and plain white paper can be used for your test stamping. Save your scrap paper for stamping excess ink off your stamps.

Tools

A variety of craft knives and cutting tools can be used for carving erasers. (See photo on page 23.) Your choice will depend upon how much detail you want in your design, and your skill in manipulating the tools. The tools you need can be found in art-supply stores, craft and hobby shops, and hardware stores. Your basic tool consists of a handle with dispos-

38. Tools needed for carving.

able or interchangeable blades. Costs vary depending upon the specific tools, yet, the cost is minimal considering that it's only the *blades* that will need to be replaced.

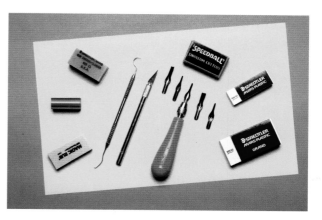

39. Tools for carving.

1. Craft Knives - Craft knives are available in several different brands. You'll want one with a thin blade for carving small and intricate shapes. For less detailed designs, you may use other blade types such as routers and gouges.

2. Linoleum Block Cutting Tools. These tools are more "heavy-duty" than most craft knives since they are meant to be used on a harder surface. Since various interchangeable blades come with the tool, however, some of them may be suitable for use on plastic erasers.

3. Scalpels. There is a scalpel available at some doll-making supply stores which is extremely sharp. You can use this tool for tiny, finely detailed areas.

Since your carving tools are sharp, protect your work surface by placing your carving-in-process on heavy cardboard or on a kitchen cutting board. Also, since the knives are very sharp, they are not suitable for use by young children. It is much safer to let a child draw a design directly onto the eraser and then have an adult carve it.

4. For drawing your designs on an eraser, use a fine-tipped, ball-point pen, a soft-lead pencil (number 2) with a sharp point, or permanent marking pens. For close, detailed work, a free-standing magnifying glass may be helpful. To pick out small bits of loose eraser from your carving block, dental tools, such as the "explorer," may be helpful. Use a small mirror for checking those designs you have carved in reverse, such as letters of the alphabet or words.

Methods and Techniques

There are several methods and techniques for carving erasers. Much will depend upon your design, your eraser and your tools.

For your first attempt at eraser carving, select a simple shape such as a triangle, a heart, a star, or a short word. To get the most mileage out of your eraser, remember that you can carve a design on each of its six sides. If a logo is printed on the eraser, you may remove it by rubbing the logo gently with a cotton ball moistened with nail polish remover or rubbing alcohol. The cleaned surface will make it easier for you to see the design while you are carving. If a logo is incised into the eraser, you may want to smooth that surface by rubbing it against fine sandpaper.

Techniques for Getting Designs onto Your Eraser

1. Drawing Technique.

Pick a simple design, such as a daisy. Using a soft-lead pencil with a good point, draw the design on the larger, flat side of your eraser. If you are pleased with the design, go over it with a permanent ink pen.

2. Tracing Technique.

40. Carved erasers by Pat Berlin.

When used only for your own artistic purposes and not for resale, you can trace pictures from newspapers and magazines to be used as designs for your stamps. If the picture is too large, you can reduce it to the size you want on a photocopy machine. Place your tracing paper over the picture and trace around it with a soft-lead pencil. Place your traced drawing face down on the eraser and, using the back of a spoon, rub gently over the entire design. That will transfer your drawing to the eraser. Lift off the tracing paper and go over the pencil lines with a pen containing permanent ink.

Often, the inks on newsprint, including the Sunday "comics," will transfer to your stamp by the rubbing method alone. The same is true for some photocopies made shortly before you want to transfer them.

Note: Letters and words create a special problem. They must be carved in reverse in order to be legible when they are stamped. To accomplish this, write or print the word on a piece of paper and transfer it to your stamp as described above, and the stamped word will read correctly.

3. Carving Techniques.

There are two basic carving techniques.

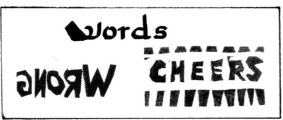

41. Carved erasers by Pat Berlin

Method A: Using a V-shaped blade from your carving tool set, and following the outline of the design, cut into the eraser, slowly and carefully,. If your design is a daisy, for example, start carving a stem, leaves, and finally the petals. The area around the design you are carving remains *uncut*. When printed on white paper, the flower will show up as white while the background shape will be the color of the ink you used.

42. Carving by Pat Berlin.

Method B: Assume you are now carving the same daisy as before. Now, however, cut away the areas that surround the stem, leaves and petals. When you print your design this time, the flower will pick up the color from your stamp pad and the background will remain white.

To put in more details, you can now go back, and using a narrow, V-shaped blade, cut a thin line between each petal to give the petals a separated look. Then cut a thin line around the center of the flower. You can also add veins to the leaves. You have now combined the techniques in both methods A and B.

Either of the methods above may be used to carve pencil erasers. Since those erasers are so small, however, the designs should be simple shapes and the carving tool should be used with the thinnest blade you have.

43. Carved words by Pat Berlin.

44. Assorted papers.

Chapter 6:

Paper

ince all papers are not created equal, the paper you use should be appropriate for what you are making. Here are some guides to help you select the best paper to use for a specific project and where can you find it.

To help you learn what kinds of paper exist, start a paper collection! Begin with writing papers, unusual colored papers, index cards or whatever you think will take a stamped image well. Ask family and friends to save interesting papers for you and watch your collection grow into a very large and varied assortment. Now comes the best part— trying your stamps on the papers you have collected. From your experimentation, you will learn what papers take an image well and which are most useful for particular purposes. You can then search out a source for those you prefer.

Plain bond paper is generally the most satisfactory paper for stamping upon and is readily available. It has a non-glossy or matte finish, which is very good for stamping since ink dries quickly on it. Glossy, or "coated" paper can also be used, but the drying time for the ink is longer. For that very reason, however, glossy papers are ideal for embossing your designs, since the embossing fluid stays wet on the surface longer, giving you more time for the embossing procedure. (See Chapter 9 on "Embossing.")

As a beginning stamper, avoid lightweight typing paper since it tends to crinkle. Also avoid "erasable" typing paper, as it smears easily.

To get the truest colors for your stamped designs, use white or lightly tinted paper. Dark papers absorb color and the stamped design may not show to advantage unless you use a much darker or lighter ink than the color of the paper.

Spread your newly stamped work on a flat surface until it is completely dry before stacking it.

Most major cities have retail and wholesale paper supply stores. You might like to begin your paper search by looking in your telephone directory's "Yellow Pages" under "Paper." You will probably find many listings and advertisements, some of which might include the brands of paper carried and their uses. If an ad does not say "Wholesale Only," the company may sell to the general public, but you should call to confirm this. Where an ad says "Cash and Carry," the store is usually open to the public. These stores usually sell such things as stationery and matching envelopes, Kraft envelopes, labels, index cards, blank business and note cards, Kraft wrapping paper, and much more. You will probably find samples to inspect, and you may be able to get samples of those which interest you. These stores often sell in larger quantities than you would be required to buy at a stationer's. The larger quantities will probably give you more paper than you need immediately or cost more than you want to spend at the moment, but eventually may result in significant savings.

In addition to the usual commercial stationery, paper stores often carry a greater variety of papers, in terms of quality, weight, and finish, than does a stationer. Heavy papers, white and colored, are standard items for most of these companies. These heavier papers are ideal for letterheads, greeting cards, and for your own creations. The heaviest of them are ideal for making bookmarks, covers for handmade books, and art pieces. Finishes on these heavier weight papers vary, so try to determine their suitability for stamping before you buy any. Carry a rubber stamp and stamp pad with you when shopping and ask the salesman for samples of those papers which interest you. With those samples in hand, try to find a quiet portion of the shop in which to make your tests.

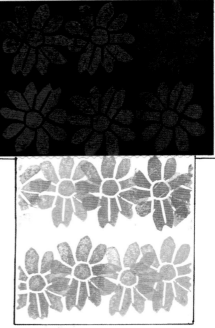

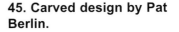

45. Carved design by Pat Berlin.

These same stores often carry blank invitations - a single flat card or a folded card with matching envelopes - in white and pastel colors. Some blank invitations have an embossed border around a center panel. On these, you can stamp over the entire card, stamp only in the center panel, or stamp only on the border.

Blank business cards are often another stock item in a commercial stationer's. They usually come 500 to a box, and can be used for gift tags, as described below.

Another intriguing item you may find is stationery with a deckled edge, which is ideal for greeting cards. When available, they are usually found boxed with matching envelopes.

Blank greeting cards found in card shops means that they are blank on the inside. For <u>completely</u> blank cards and matching envelopes, you'll probably have to go to an art supply shop or stationery store. Some of those blank cards are made from watercolor paper and have a deckled edge, others are of plainer stock. Such cards are ideal to paint on but may be too textured to take a good impression from a stamp containing fine details. You can get around that problem

46. Carved stamps by Pat Berlin.

47. Stamped collage by Kathy Amt.

by stamping your design on a separate piece of paper and then carefully tacking it to the front of the card with a touch of white glue at each corner. This is how pictures are inserted into some fine art books, a procedure called "tipping in."

Gift tags can be made from a variety of papers, but the stock should be thicker than bond paper to prevent them from wrinkling. Blank business cards are an ideal size and weight for gift tags. They usually come in white but can also be found in pastel colors. Heavy-weight papers, as described previously, can also be cut into tag size cards. If you have a paper cutter and cut just one sheet at a time, your edges will stay smooth. If you don't have a paper cutter, use a flat, metal ruler and a fresh blade in a craft knife to cut out your tags. You can also cut up unlined index cards to make gift tags. Most index cards are white, but they can often be found in pastel colors.

To finish a gift tag, punch a hole at the top and insert a string or a narrow ribbon. The standard hole punch has a one-quarter inch hole, but punches with smaller holes are available and the smaller holes are a more appropriate

48. Carved stamp designs by Pat Berlin.

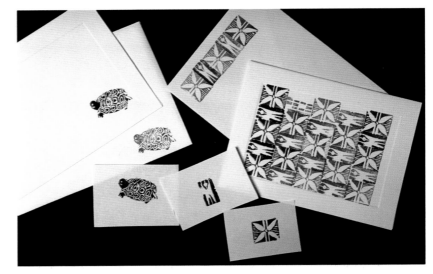

49. Carved designs by Jamie Brooks.

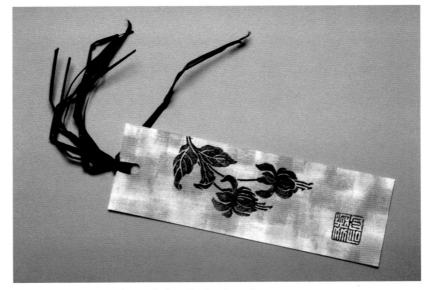

50. Stamped bookmark by Judy Jacobs.

size for a tag. Also, there are many punches in the stores today which punch out hearts, stars and a variety of other shapes, any of which may add interest to your work.

Make your own labels. Adhesive labels are every-where, from the stationer to the art supply store and the stationery section of some large drug stores! Blank labels come in many shapes and sizes and are packaged with varying numbers of sheets to a package. It's a good idea to stamp an entire sheet of labels before peeling them off as they are needed since it is faster to stamp an entire sheet at one time than to peel off one label at a time, place it on an envelope and then stamp it. Sheets with just one, full-page label, are also available, and can be used to cover a tin or a box.

With a little imagination, you can make gift wrapping paper. Plain Kraft paper takes stamping well, and paper suppliers, as well as some art supply stores, sell it by the roll. White "butcher's paper" and shelf lining paper also come in rolls and may be used to create decorated wrapping paper.

If you plan to make your own gift wrapping paper, consider using rubber stamps

51. Labels by Pat Berlin.

52. Roller Stamp.

mounted on a roller. With this, you just run your roller across your stamp pad, place it on the paper, and go. The roller method is fast, especially on large areas.

And ribbon! Some ribbons will take a stamped image better than others, and the image will not smear. While greeting card shops often carry ribbons, your local fabric store may have a larger selection and may allow you to buy them in smaller quantities. You can also make your own "ribbon" out of the same paper you used for your gift wrap. Cut a length long enough to go around the package plus an inch or so for overlap, so that you can tape or glue your paper ribbon to the bottom of the package.

Exotic papers can be purchased at some art supply stores and through catalogs. (See the "Resources" section.) Some companies specializing in handmade papers offer, for a nominal fee, a sampling of the papers they make or carry . The samples are small, but generally give you enough surface to stamp on.

Among the exotic papers are Japanese rice papers. Some are very strong and are sold in large sheets. The sheets do not tear easily and cutting

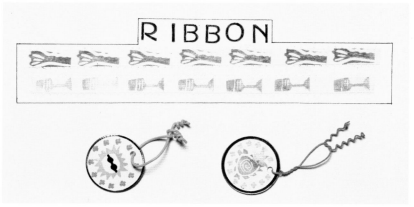

53. Stamping by Pat Berlin.

54. Stamping by Pat Berlin.

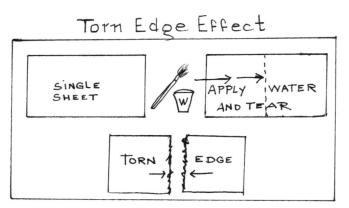

55. Torn edge effect.

them with scissors or a blade is not appropriate to their handmade look. Here's an easy solution for dividing a large sheet into smaller pieces. Wet a clean paint-brush with clean water. "Paint" a line where you want to divide the paper. Do this several times until the paper is well saturated. Then, with the paper flat on a table and with one hand on each side of the wet dividing line, pull the paper apart. The tear line will be jagged, like the deckling on other fancy papers.

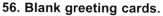

56. Blank greeting cards.

Once you have your pieces separated, place a sheet of clean, blank paper over each section and weight them down with a book, so that the wet edges will be completely flat when they dry. Let the paper dry completely before handling it. If the divided sheets are too large to store easily, divide them further.

Paper, and its use in stamping, is a big topic. I have offered some observations and suggestions as to paper weight, color, availability, and appropriate uses of paper as it relates to hand stamping. As usual, I urge you to experiment! That is part of the fun, and challenge, of stamping.

57. Blank note cards.

58. Stationery and calendar envelopes.

Chapter 7:

Don't Stop With Paper!

Try These Themes and Variations

A Medium for the Message

I find it difficult to browse in a card store without buying many of the cards I see. Admittedly, the artistry, verse and humor of some of the better cards are superb, but why compare them to a card you make? A personally made card, whether it is on construction paper, cardboard, or handmade paper, is always preferable. It is always "good enough" because it is totally original and, more to the point, it is heartfelt.

The easiest card to make is one made of paper. A single sheet of paper can be folded in any direction, cut into any shape, painted on, sponged on, sewn on, and of course, rubber-stamped on.

Now, try being a "Whatiffer." A "Whatiffer" might ask: "What if I made a card shaped like a slice of pizza and decorated it? What if I then cut circles out of red felt for pepperoni slices? And for a finishing touch, "What if I made an envelope like a miniature pizza box?"

For a different occasion, a "Whatiffer" might ask, "What if I made some doodle drawings on a piece of paper, then, using a sewing machine, stitched all over it, leaving some threads dangling down, each thread having a tiny bead at the end?"

A "Whatiffer", getting carried away by the wealth of her ideas, might ask, "What if I took a long piece of paper, folded it like a fan, and stamped each fan section differently? What if I then wrote a story or a poem on the other side?"

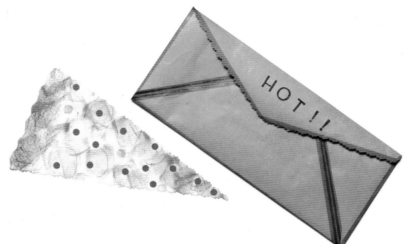

59. By Pat Berlin.

How about decorating "goody" bags for a birthday party, or better yet, let the children decorate the bags themselves as part of the party activities? Bags may even be personalized. Lunch can be brightened too, with decorated lunch bags personalized with the muncher's name.

Do you enjoy jigsaw puzzles? Stamp your own designs on blank, pre-cut puzzles, or make your own puzzles.

If you want to mail your creation, and it is not a standard size, make your own envelope or mailer. Remember, though, that the minimum envelope size for the U. S. Postal Service is 3" by 5".

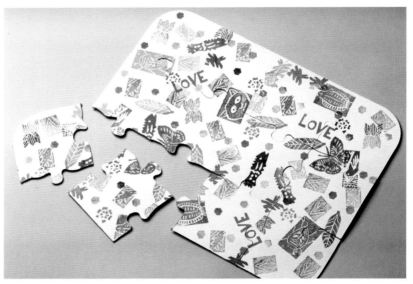

60. Commercial blank puzzle - stamped by Pat Berlin.

Instead of Rubber Stamps

Any object that can be placed on an ink pad can be used as if it were a rubber stamp. Stones, ceramic pieces, old jewelry, pieces of wood, buttons, potatoes, and corks can all be used. The surface of the object must be able to accept and hold the ink, and must be fairly flat in order to print evenly. A curved object, such as a cylinder bead, can be rolled for inking and printing. This imaginative means of creating art is especially appealing to children of all ages. Do not forget that you are using ink. It may be hard, if not impossible, to remove the ink residue from objects such as unfired ceramics, jewelry or wood, so make sure these off-beat stamps are either cleanable or disposable.

Sponges can be used in a variety of ways. An ordinary, synthetic household sponge can be cut into such shapes as animals, flowers, geometrics, etc. Large kitchen shears work best for cutting these sponges. You may find low-cost, pre-cut sponges at your local craft store. There are also odd-shaped natural sponges which can be used for stamping, but they can be expensive. Make-up sponges, though they have smaller pores, are also good for stamping.

Aside from cutting out shapes from sponges, a sponge may be used to create a background area, over which further stamping can be done. When used to provide a background pattern, the sponge should be lightly inked and applied to the paper with a light touch.

Let's say that you want to create an underwater background. First stamp a light background of pale blue, then go over the same area with a light green. It is usually best to rotate the sponge 90 degrees with each stamping for a varied effect. Depending upon the degree of darkness you want, the sponge may or may not need to be re-inked each time you stamp. You can also lighten the color by "stamping off" some ink on paper towels before stamping on your paper. Keep the used sponges for craft work only.

If children are doing the stamping, I suggest that you have them use water-soluble stamp-pad ink or water-soluble paint for stamping on paper. This precaution will make the final clean-up easier. When permanence is required, as it would be when stamping on fabric, use inks or paints specifically made for fabrics since they are designed for use on items that will be laundered.

61. Found objects used as stamps.

62. Foam rubber shapes.

63. various sponges.

64. Sponge stamping and fish stamp by Pat Berlin.

65. Stamped collage by Judy Jacobs.

Chapter 8:

Who Was That Masked Stamp?

 n creating stamped designs, there may be times when you'll want to combine two or more stamped images, or to remove part of an image. This can be done easily by "masking," or "blocking out" a portion of the stamp you want to use. With this technique, and its variations, you can bring new and unusual creativity to your work.

The first and easiest "blocking out" technique involves "layering." In this process, one or more of the stamped images will appear behind the others. Perhaps you would like a row of apples with the second apple behind and partly hidden by the first one, the third apple behind and slightly hidden by the second, and so on. To accomplish this, you will need to make a "mask." First, stamp the apple image on a piece of scrap, light weight bond paper. With a pair of sharp scissors, cut the apple from the paper exactly along its outside edge. Do not leave any margin outside the apple, or narrow spaces will show on your successive stampings. You may need to cut out finer images with a craft knife.

When you have your mask ready, put it aside, re-ink your stamp and print the apple again, but this time on your good paper. When you are sure the ink is dry, place your mask exactly over the apple you have just stamped. Re-ink your stamp and gently stamp the second apple over the first, BUT a bit to one side and slightly higher than the preceding apple. When you finish, it will appear that one apple is behind the other.

You can mask any stamped image. To go back to the apple example, suppose you want a variety of fruit in a row. Stamp and mask your apple. Now stamp an orange slightly overlapping the apple. Then mask the orange and stamp a banana slightly overlapping the orange. The stamped images do not have to be the same size. Just be sure your masks fit exactly and that you position your stamp appropriately before stamping.

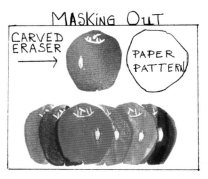

66. Stamps hard carved by Pat Berlin.

Masking is also a handy technique when you want to create an illusion of depth or distance. You can give an illusion of greater depth and distance to a stand of trees, for example, if you use the masking technique and simultaneously reduce the amount of pressure applied to your stamps. Here's how to do it. Stamp the closest tree, then mask it when it is dry. Re-ink your stamp and, with a little less pressure than before, stamp the second tree slightly behind the first one. The second tree will be a little lighter than the first one. Continue in this manner until you have the number of trees you want, and the proper degree of dark to light to give the feeling of depth. The first, or closest tree, will be the darkest. The last, and lightest tree, will appear to be the farthest away.

67. Hand carved stamps by Pat Berlin.

There are other ways to vary the intensity, or the lightness or darkness, of an image. You can reduce the intensity of an image by stamping two or more images from the same stamp before re-inking it. Later images will be lighter than the earlier ones. You can also lighten an image by stamping off some ink on scrap paper before using that stamp on your work. Much will depend on the design itself, the wetness of your pad, the amount of ink on your stamp, and the pressure you use in stamping. Practicing on scrap paper will help you get all these variables under control.

68. Hand carved stamps by Pat Berlin.

Instant transplants can be made and you are the surgeon. Any form — human, animal, or object — can have a change of head or body part by masking out one part or another. The many combinations can be endless, and very amusing.

What if you want to block out a small part of a larger image? Let's assume that you have a stamp with a heart design on it, for example, but you want to show a broken heart. Simple! Cut out a crack shape from scrap paper. Ink your stamp and, using tweezers if necessary, carefully lay the *uninked* crack over the inked heart on the stamp and then stamp it, crack and

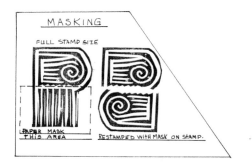

69. Hand carved stamps by Pat Berlin.

all. The ink will hold the crack to the heart and you will have produced a broken heart.

There are many other ways this basic method can be used. For example, a stamp may have a border that you would like to use around another design. Stamp the bordered image on scrap paper as the first step in creating a mask. Carefully cut out everything but the border, then place the mask over that central part of your stamp. There is now a frame waiting to be filled with a design of your choosing.

Sections of large stamps can be masked in the same way. You may, for example, remove one person or object from a group.

A mask can be used over and over again and can be considered a "pattern piece." After much use, however, you may find that the mask has become saturated with old inks and these inks may transfer through the paper to the image it is masking. You might think that using heavy paper or cardboard for a mask would increase its usefulness, but a thick mask can mean that your stamp may not ink the paper directly around the masked image, resulting in a slight halo around your image the same color as your paper. For the same reason, it is important to make sure you cut out the mask on the outside image lines, with no white paper around the mask image. Since masks are easy to make, do not continually re-use a mask since it may eventually give you problems. If you plan on using the same mask frequently, cut out several of them at the same time.

As you become more skilled at masking your stamps, you will probably accumulate many masks. I like to store my masks in plastic page protectors and keep them in a three-ring binder. You can also store masks in labeled envelopes, or in self-locking, plastic bags. You can stamp the design on the envelope or label it. As your collection of masks grows, you might want to divide them by subject and file the envelopes in file folders.

Masking is yet another technique that gives increased versatility to your stamping and life to your stamp art. It is fun and interesting to do, and will make people wonder how you created your work.

70. Hand carved stamps by Pat Berlin.

71. Commercial stamp, showing paper mask.

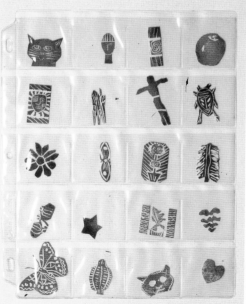

72. Plastic sleeve holder for patterns.

73. Stamped, embossed and hole punched card designs by Pat Berlin.

Chapter 9:

Embossing

ow attractive and elegant a hand stamped greeting card, invitation or letterhead looks when embossed! The raised surface and the shiny look can add a whole new dimension to your creation.

The raised effect is obtained by using an embossing fluid on your stamp, rather than ink. After you stamp your design with the embossing fluid, the still wet image is coated with an embossing powder. Then, the powder is heated until it rises and hardens.

Here is what you'll need to emboss your designs: an uninked stamp pad, embossing fluid, embossing powder, a small brush and a heat source. The embossing fluid is a thick, clear liquid. The embossing powders, on the other hand, come in a variety of colors. Your paper should be standard weight or heavier since very thin paper might burn in the heating process.

For the best results, be sure that your stamps are clean and free from ink before you use them for embossing. To make an embossed design, saturate your uninked stamp pad with embossing fluid and then stamp your design. Now sprinkle embossing powder over the still wet design. The powder will adhere to the embossing fluid. To remove excess powder, gently tap your stamped design over a piece of scrap paper so that the excess powder will fall onto it. To reuse that powder, fold the paper into a spout and pour the powder back into its container. Use a small dry brush to remove any unwanted particles still remaining on the stamped design.

As mentioned earlier, heat causes the powder to rise and harden. There are many sources of heat you can use in the embossing process. The best and safest is a heat gun, which can be bought at craft shops. An ordinary hair dryer does not produce enough heat for this process.

When using a heat gun, aim the gun at the surface of your art work, at the distance recommended by the manufacturer. The art work can be hand held or placed flat on a table. When the powder starts to melt, it will look shiny and that is the time to remove your art work from the heat. **Embossing is not a method recommended for children, even when supervised. Let adults emboss the designs the children have created.**

If you want to autograph your work and emboss it, write your name with a ball point pen containing erasable ink. The ink in those pens stays wet long enough for the embossing powder to adhere to it. Add your embossing powder and heat it as described above.

As with most things worth doing, embossing requires practice. Don't get discouraged if your first attempts aren't perfect. Use scrap paper for your early attempts

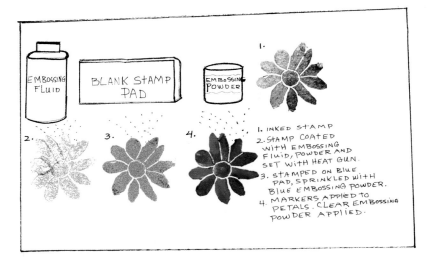

74. By Pat Berlin.

75. Commercial stamp, gold embossed.

and work your way up to greeting cards and invitations!

Double Embossing

Double embossing is a technique which will allow you to obtain some particularly interesting effects. In double embossing, emboss your design exactly as I've described above. After it has cooled, restamp the same design, but offset it slightly from the original stamping. Now, change the color of your embossing powder, then heat and set it.

In the piece pictured, I chose a simple feather design with incised lines. On a black paper base, I stamped three feathers in a row, each about a quarter of an inch from its neighbor. I then coated the feathers with a light colored embossing powder, and heated the powder to set it. After the embossed picture had cooled for a few seconds, I restamped the feathers, each just a bit away from the previous ones. I then coated the new images with a darker embossing powder and heated the second images to set the powder. For the third stamping, I used a gold embossing powder. The effect was three dimensional and striking. If you use just two shades of the same color, you can get the effect of shadows.

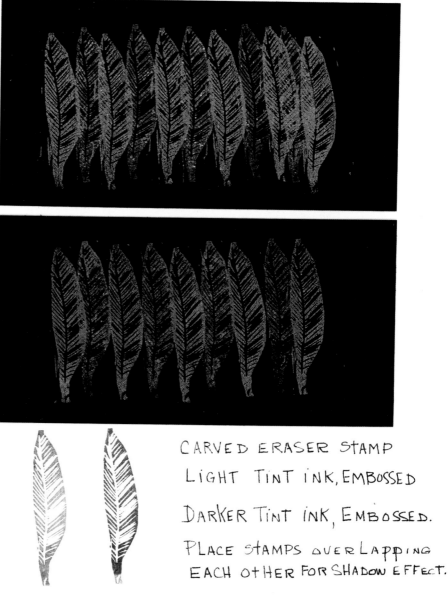

CARVED ERASER STAMP
LIGHT TINT INK, EMBOSSED
DARKER TINT INK, EMBOSSED.
PLACE STAMPS OVERLAPPING
EACH OTHER FOR SHADOW EFFECT.

76. Stamping by Pat Berlin.

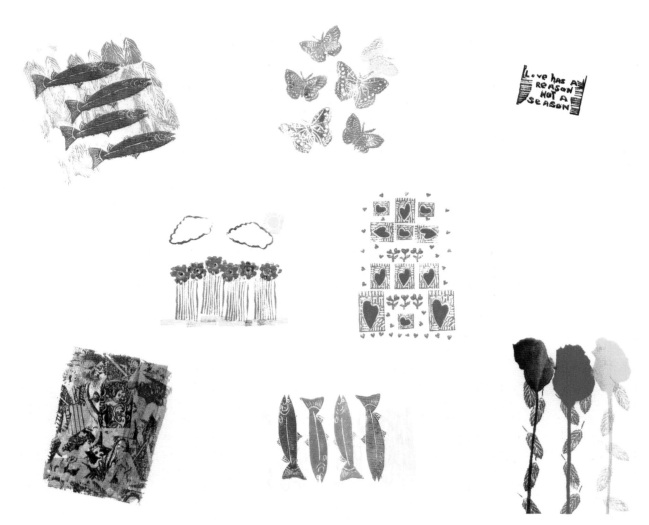

77. The original stampings that make up this image were taken to a specialized copy shop and reduced to 25% of their original size on a color copier. When they were at the right size, they were cut apart and arranged on white paper. They were again copied on a color copier and the result is above. The above image was also copied onto a transparent acetate.

Chapter 10:

Stamping, Laser Printers and Photocopiers

et's say that you'd like to carve a feather on an eraser, but your drawing ability is minimal. Don't fret - a photocopying machine can help you. The ink on a photocopy dries slowly enough so that the image can be transferred from it to an eraser and become a guide for your carving. Here's how to do it. Place a real feather, or a picture of one, on the photocopier and close the cover. If your feather is larger than the stamp you wish to carve, the copy machine may be able to reduce the size of the copy it creates. If it can, make one or more reductions until you get the size you want. If the photocopier cannot make reductions, find one that can. To save time and money in photocopying, you can copy as many items at one time as will fit on a standard sheet of paper, or as will fit on an even larger sheet, if the machine can accommodate it.

Now, cut out the copy you made of the feather and place it, ink side down, onto your eraser. It is best to transfer the copied feather within a day or two of making it, or the ink may dry out and will not transfer. Take a cotton swab or cotton ball, dampen it slightly with nail polish remover, and rub it over the back of the picture slowly, evenly, and carefully. (When working with nail polish remover, it is a good idea to do so in a well ventilated room and to wear rubber gloves.)

Once you have done this, gently lift one corner to see how clearly the feather has transferred to the eraser. If it did not transfer well, continue rubbing. After the transfer is complete, remove the paper and throw it away. The ink will not transfer a second time because it has been exhausted. If necessary, go over the image with a fine-point marker, or a fine-tip pen, containing permanent ink. The eraser can now be carved.

Larry Thomas of Atlanta, Georgia, is a stamper who really gets a lot of mileage from the photocopier. He uses images from hand-carved erasers and commercially made rubber stamps to create interesting artwork. Sometimes he also uses images made from his collection of personal and found photographs. The photographs are enlarged or reduced on the photocopier, as desired. When the picture is transferred to the eraser, certain areas are carved away. This leaves other areas, such as the eyes, the mouth and hair, "up" (above the background), ready to take the ink from the pad or markers. A second eraser is then carved from a second photocopy of the same image. This time the positive areas which were left "up" before, such as the eyes, the mouth and hair, are now cut away. The first eraser may be stamped with one color and

78. By Larry Thomas.

the second eraser with a different color. Of course, the images need to be lined up exactly for the best results.

Stamps made by using this photocopy transfer process are quite interesting and totally unique. Some photocopy shops have self-service copy machines with reduction and enlargement capabilities. This allows you to experiment entirely on your own with both the size and the darkness of the copies you make. Photocopying can be addictive. Make sure you have enough change before you start.

79. Corel Draw!™ comes with thousands of clip art images which can be used for stamping.

Laser Printer

This photocopier transfer technique works equally well with laser printers. If you have a laser printer attached to your computer, almost any type of computer graphic can be used as a guide for stamp carving. Laser printers print in virtually the same way as do photocopiers, so the ink will transfer well onto an eraser.

Using a computer will open up a whole new world of stamping design for you. The simplest way to get started is to use the paint program that came with your computer. Just draw a pattern on your computer and print it. If you need to make the picture larger or smaller to better fit your eraser, your paint program will let you make it the size you want.

Another benefit that computers bring to stamping is the abundance of computer clip art you can use. Programs like Corel Draw!™ come with thousands of clip art images. CD-ROMs full of clip art are inexpensive and available from your local computer store. Just about any piece of computer clip art can be modified or used as is as a guide for carving a rubber stamp.

ThinK ART

ThinK ART

ThinK ART

80. Use a photocopier to make your design various sizes.

81. Hand painted and stamped envelope by Judy Jacobs.

Chapter 11:

Stamp Out Boring Mail!

 appily for stamping enthusiasts, envelopes have much unused space, thereby giving you an opportunity to brighten up the mail.

White or lightly tinted envelopes having a matte surface are the best on which to stamp. Highly textured envelopes may not provide a flat enough surface to show off your stamping very well, and glossy envelopes are prone to smearing. Once you become experienced, you might like to work on post cards, Kraft envelopes, boxes, mailing tubes, or any container that travels through the mail.

Leave ample space for the address and postage, and decorate around these areas. In addition to stamping, you can create a collage over certain sections. Keep your decorations on the front of the envelope so as not to confuse the canceling machine and thus delay your letter. Mail art runs the risk of being damaged when going through these machines. If you are concerned about this, you may take your letter to the post office and have it hand canceled.

If you are "mail-art lonely," there are many stampers, clubs and groups who enjoy exchanging mail art. People often advertise in rubber stamp periodicals and it is easy to find someone with whom to correspond and exchange artwork.

Requests for "mail art" entries into exhibitions and shows occur with some frequency. The regulations are reasonably unrestricted as to the size of the items to be submitted, and sometimes there is a theme to the exhibit.

One of the earliest pieces of rubber-stamped mail carried a simple message, "STAMP OUT BORING MAIL!" Let's all help.

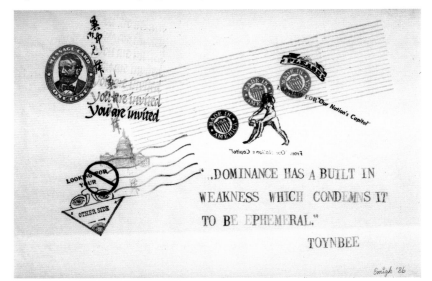

82. Stamped envelope by Kathy Amt.

83. Stamped post card by Pat Berlin.

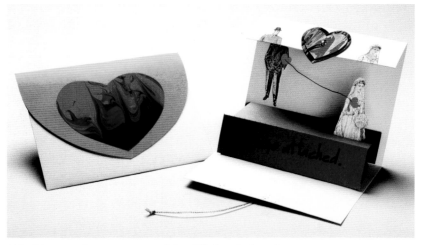

84. Stamped pop-up card by Michael Jacobs.

85. Stamped stationery, envelopes with faux stamps and calendar art envelopes by Pat Berlin.

86. Discarded calendar pages folded into envelopes with a stamped label added, by Pat Berlin.

Chapter 12:

Carved Stamps, Recycling and Hand-made Envelopes

hat do you do when you tire of some of your hand-carved erasers? How do you dispose of all that junk mail you get? What do you do with magazine pictures and used greeting cards? Recycle them! All of them can be given a new life and be put to good use.

Carved Stamps

After using a favored eraser stamp for many months, I sometimes get tired of the design. Here's how to give new life to those old designs.

Place some large sheets of blank paper on your work surface and spread those eraser stamps that need rejuvenation in front of you. Since you'll be concentrating on design rather than color, stamp all the designs with black ink. Now look at the designs you stamped and decide how you would like to alter them. Suggestions follow.

1. You can make a design more detailed by making additional cuts into it. If your stamp contains the shape of a broad leaf, for example, you can add more veins to the leaf by making additional cuts in it. Similarly, you can add more rays to a sun by making additional cuts in the eraser.

2. If you want to simplify the design, cut away previously carved areas you no longer want. You can remove all the leaves and the stem of a flower, for example, leaving just the flower blossom.

3. You can change the design by cutting the eraser in half. Before cutting into your stamp, mark your cutting line with a pen containing permanent ink. Use a sharp bladed knife to cut on that line. (If the eraser has been carved on both sides, remember that you will be cutting both designs in half.) You can further alter the design by cutting each of those halves in half, etc. This "cutting down" is most effective on geometric and abstract designs and may be too disruptive on a design such as a landscape.

BEFORE AND AFTER LEAF SHAPE ERASERS.

87. By Pat Berlin.

Recycling

Recycling certainly helps our environment, and can also be fun. As a start, save business reply envelopes you receive in the mail, even though they may have a logo or other printing on them. You can cover the printing with a collage or a blank piece of paper. Michael Jacobs, a master at recycling, teaches and uses this method very successfully. It's always fun to receive mail from him. Much of it is in recycled envelopes or on packages and covered with stamping and collage. {See page 76.)

I keep a large carton for throwaways I think I might successfully recycle. In it I put parts of brochures and junk mail, calendars, greeting cards, and pages from magazines.

You can add stamping to interesting brochures or magazine pages. Go ahead and stamp a crocodile by the swimming pool on that vacation brochure or add a couple of penguins to that desert scene! Let your imagination run wild.

Many of the brochures, and most of the magazines today, are printed on glossy paper. Stamping on such paper requires the use of permanent inks, not water-based ones. Even then, you must give your stamping time to dry to avoid having the ink smear.

Hand-made Envelopes

Large sheets of printed material, such as a full-page picture from a magazine or a scene from a calendar, can be recycled and made into very interesting envelopes which may then be stamped or used as the base of a collage. Simply fold the sheet in half or into thirds and seal the edges with transparent tape.

If you feel the need for the look of a commercially made envelope, however, you can duplilcate that look. To do so, make a pattern for your envelope by carefully peeling open an appropriately sized envelope or by steaming the envelope open over a kettle of boiling water until the glue softens. Then, open the flaps and flatten them out so that you can see how the envelope was constructed. With the help of a ruler, mark the fold lines and where the flaps overlapped for gluing. This will give you a pattern for the envelopes you will make yourself. If you'd like a sturdier pattern or template, place the flattened envelope on a piece of cardboard or acetate and trace around it. Then, as before, draw in the fold and overlap lines. Cut your template out of the cardboard or acetate with scissors or a craft knife.

To create your own envelope, lay your template over a magazine page or calendar scene, trace around the edges of your template, and then cut the tracing out with scissors. Fold the new envelope into its final form, and seal it together with craft glue or use gummed stickers along the seams. Make sure the glue is dry before using the envelope. If your envelope is made of glossy paper, use permanent inks on your stamps and allow time for your stamping to dry. Also, if there is no clear space for the address, place an adhesive label on the envelope for that purpose. Craft glue should also be used on the back of your postage stamp to keep the stamp from sliding off the glossy paper!

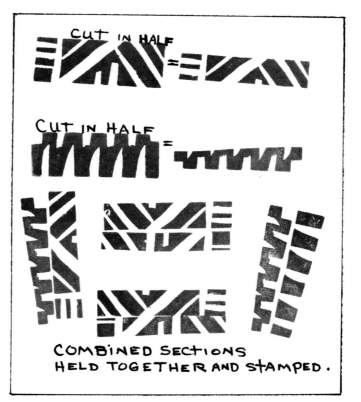

88. Carved erasers by Pat Berlin.

Great Impressions: The Art and Technique of Rubber Stamping

89. Stamped border on mat board, by Pat Berlin.

58

Chapter 13:

Displaying Your Creations

roper matting and framing can enhance your artwork greatly. You can use a plain, unadorned mat, keeping in mind that its color should complement the work being matted. How exciting it would be, though, if you extended your artwork to include the mat that will surround it. In that case, you will also need to make sure that the color of the mat is light enough so that your stamping will show.

Much of your work will probably fit into pre-cut mats which come in a variety of colors and sizes. To stamp your mat, start at one corner and stamp all around the mat until you return to your starting point. If, however, you want a balanced look, start by stamping in the same position in each corner. Then stamp in the middle of each side. Stamp again in the middle of the remaining spaces, etc.

Be careful not to smudge your work by dragging your sleeve across it. Also, be sure that your stamping is dry before working in another area. If you want more than one line of images around your border, plan the spacing for those lines before you start. Ideally it's best to finish your first line before starting the next. You have several choices when creating borders. You can use the same design for each border, a different design for each border, several designs combined to make a border, etc. The choice is yours.

Borders and mats may be embellished further. Anything that can be glued down can be added to the mat - beads, silk or paper flowers, ribbon, shells, ticket stubs, pieces of discarded mail, parts of postcards, and even coins. Making a collage of such things is easy and errors in stamping can be neatly covered over by what you glue over them. It is best to arrange your non-stamp items on the mat to see how they will look before gluing them down. A white craft glue is usually adequate for affixing most items.

Now that your mat is finished, the question is, "To frame, or not to frame?" There are a large number of reasonably priced, ready made frames available. They come in plastic, metal, all-glass, and wood and in many standard sizes. There are also inexpensive plastic "box" frames in a variety of sizes. All-glass or hard plastic frames are very suitable for framing stamp art, especially art that does not need a mat. Choose a frame appropriate to the style and feeling of the artwork. Your art should not be cramped in its frame, nor should the frame detract from the art.

If you want to frame your work, and can find a ready-made frame you like, you'll have little trouble framing it yourself. If you have created a three-dimensional collage, however, framing may be somewhat more difficult and costly, since you will need a frame designed to accommodate the thickness of your work. In that case, you might want to ask for guidance from someone working in a framing shop.

Assuming that your work is flat and you want to frame it yourself, place your frame face down on the table. If your artwork will be protected by glass, place the glass in the frame. Then, place your mat face down on top of the glass. The next layer is your artwork, which is placed face down on top of the mat and taped into position, if necessary. Lastly, a piece of light cardboard, which generally comes with your frame, is placed over your artwork and held into place with the small nails or staples provided..

To protect your unframed art work, use a clear protective coating on the picture to keep it from becoming soiled. This can be done with a material called a fixative, which can be found at most art supply stores. Commercial fixatives vary — there are types for charcoal and pastels, and others for watercolors. Choose one recommended for watercolors. In a pinch, hair-spray will do!

90. Krylon Crystal Clear spray, fixative.

91. Krylon Dulling Spray, fixative.

Apply the fixative before matting. The fixative produces a fine mist coating which protects the artwork from soil and moisture. Spraying of fixatives is best done outdoors on a windless day or in a sheltered area, or in a well-ventilated room. To "fix" the artwork, lay it out flat and follow the directions on the can, which will tell you the recommended distance at which to hold the spray can.

Spray the mist evenly to avoid having the fixative puddle or streak. A slow, even, back-and-forth motion works well. Allow the piece to dry completely before working with it some more.

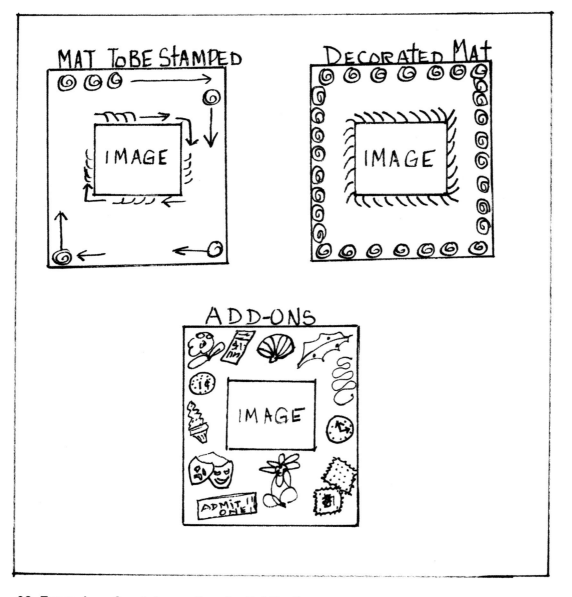

92. Examples of mat decoration, by Pat Berlin.

93. Stamped and laminated paper dangle earrings, by Pat Berlin.

Chapter 14:

Making Paper Jewelry with Stamped Images

ot only is it simple, but it is quite inexpensive to produce earrings and necklaces out of paper, a plastic laminate, and easily available jewelry mountings. You can make jewelry to complement any outfit or to serve as unique and interesting gifts.

First, choose a paper that has some stiffness to it. Light-weight watercolor paper, unlined index cards, and bristol or poster board make a fine base for paper jewelry. Poster board comes in a variety of weights and colors, and can be found at your local art supply store. Paper that wrinkles easily will not be suitable for making jewelry.

To start, choose a design from your collection of stamps for use on a pair of earrings. Then, stamp that design on scrap paper and try different shapes around it such as a circle, a diamond, a square, or a teardrop, etc. Select the shape you like best. Next, stamp your design onto your good paper. Assuming you want identical earrings, draw identical shapes around each design. You can use coins for round shapes, or ready-made templates for other shapes. Templates containing a variety of shapes may be found in craft shops.

If you made a free-hand drawing of the shape to be used for your earrings, fold the paper on which it is drawn and cut out two shapes simultaneously. If you want a design to show on both sides of the earring, stamp the back of each earring after the first side is dry. If you use heavy paper, your designs will not show through from one side to the other. Let your earrings dry completely before continuing.

Next, laminate your earrings to protect them and make them more durable. You can buy clear plastic laminating sheets at most office and art supply stores. Cut out a piece of the laminating sheet a bit larger than your earrings. Peel off the backing paper from the laminating sheet and place your earring face down onto it. Turn your earring over and laminate that side as well. With sharp scissors, cut off the excess laminate.

Now you have to decide how to mount your earrings. Craft shops, and many art supply stores, carry what are called jewelry "findings," the "hardware" needed to complete the earrings. There are several types of earrings that are simple to make. Two types of findings for pierced ears are "posts" and "ear wires" Findings for non-pierced ears are called "screwbacks" and "clip-ons."

Earrings with posts are worn close to the ears. The posts have a flat pad at one end to which you glue your earring shapes. Before gluing them together, roughen both the pad and the laminate with fine sandpaper, so that they will have a better surface for holding the glue. Then, using a small amount of an epoxy glue, affix the flat pad to the back of the earring. You can center the pad on the design, or at the top of it, depending upon the size of the earring and how it is to be worn.

A dangle earring can be made by using an ear wire. Using a one eighth inch hole punch, make a hole at the top of each earring, but not so close to the edge as to weaken it. Punch the hole in the same position in each earring. At the bottom of

EARRING SHAPES

ABSTRACT SHAPE-STAMPED. FOLD TOGETHER ON DOTTED LINE, GLUE BOTH SIDES TO FORM ONE EARRING - DESIGN IS NOW ON BOTH SIDES. REPEAT FOR SECOND EARRING.

94. By Pat Berlin.

the ear wire is a loop. With a pair of small pliers, carefully bend a part of the loop to one side, giving you just enough of an opening to get the earring onto the loop. When that is done, bend back the open loop to close it. Repeat these steps to assemble the second earring and you will then have a pair of dangling earrings!

Clip-on earring backs come in a variety of styles and sizes. Choose a style appropriate to your earring design. For clip-on earrings, you affix the earrings to pads as described above for post earrings. Again, roughen the pad surfaces and the laminate with sandpaper for better adhesion.

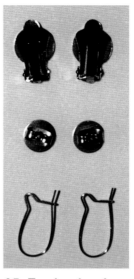

95. Earring hardware and findings.

Other jewelry findings include brooch and barrette backings which come in a variety of shapes and sizes. Brooches, or pins, and barrettes can be assembled in the same way as post earrings. Choose a backing appropriate to the size of the brooch or barrette you wish to make and one that is slightly smaller than the finished piece. Too small a backing will be flimsy and might pull off.

To finish a pendant, you can either:

1. Punch two small holes near the top edge of the pendant, run a thin cord, ribbon, or leather thong through those holes, and tie the ends together at the back to give you the length you want, or

2. Punch one small hole near the top center of the pendant and use a jump ring to connect your pendant to a cord or ribbon. A jump ring is a circular wire with a split in it and it comes in an assortment of sizes. You will need one which is large enough to accommodate the top of the pendant and the cord that you are using, with enough space left over for the pendant to hang freely. Open the jump ring by gently twisting it from side to side. Put the pendant and the cord into the open ring, then twist the ring back to close it. If you pull the jump ring open, you may not be able to get it to close securely.

You can make a necklace from a series of laminated, stamped shapes, such as graduated circles. Assemble such necklaces by following either of the methods described above for pendants. If you prefer, punch holes at the sides of each segment and connect the segments together with jump rings. Beads with holes large enough to accommodate a cord can also be added.

You can buy leather thongs and colorful silk cords where they sell findings, and at some fabric shops. Stores with findings often sell metal chain by the inch, too. If you want to use chain, remember to buy the clasps you'll need for it.

Bracelet blanks are also available at some craft shops. These blanks have blank flat pads between the links on which buttons, beads or stamped work can be affixed with an epoxy glue.

In the next chapter you'll find some ideas for combining stamping with polymer clay to create other unique jewelry.

96. Bracelet by Terry Foreman. Hand stamped design on fabric, painted and stitched.

97. Carved eraser by Pat Berlin.

98. Carved eraser stamped on paper, laminated and made into dangle earrings, by Pat Berlin.

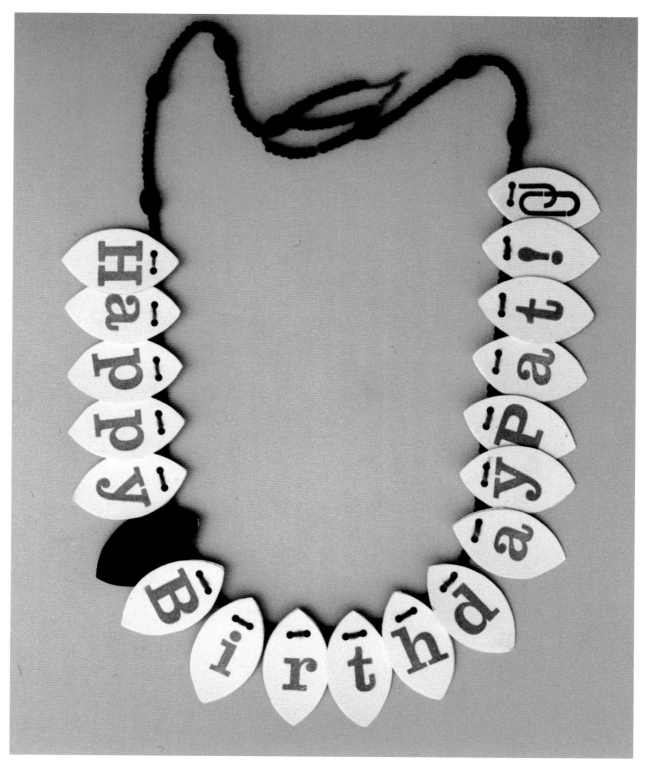

99. Birthday necklace by Nancy Johnson.

100. Stamped designs on polymer clay.

Chapter 15:

Polymer Clay and Stamp Art

ave you had the pleasure of working with polymer clay? Beautiful, colorful, durable beads, buttons, jewelry, wall tiles, refrigerator magnets, switch plates and many other objects may be made with polymer clay — and the clay can be stamped, too.

Polymer clay is sometimes referred to as a modeling compound. Among its assets is that it can be hardened in a short time by baking it at low temperatures. If you haven't investigated this material yet, I suggest you look at the books available on the subject, especially **The New Clay** by Nan Roche. An entirely new, exciting world may open for you.

Since my focus in this book is on rubber stamping, the directions which follow are brief and aimed at those people who already know how to work with the polymer clays.

Let's assume that you'd like to make a polymer clay pendant with a stamped design on it. Here's how to do it. Roll the clay to a thickness of about one-eighth of an inch. Select a stamp and ink it with a permanent ink, not a water-based one. Use a color that will both look well and show up well against the clay background you are using. Gently press that stamp onto the rolled-out clay, using enough even pressure to transfer the image well, but not so much as to flatten the clay too much. If you want to press an image into the clay but don't want any color, just use a very clean, un-inked stamp. The clay can also be impressed with objects such as buttons, antique jewelry, and medals.

After the design is transferred to the clay, decide on the size and shape of your pendant, then cut out that shape with a sharp knife, a cookie-cutter or, for long even cuts, a pizza cutter. (Those kitchen utensils used in working with polymer clay should not be used afterwards in food preparation.)

David Edwards is a very talented and prolific polymer clay artist. For designing on polymer clay, he often uses printer's type, children's lettering sets, and natural objects. On some of his stamped pieces, he applies acrylic paint over the lettering, then lightly sands the piece to remove all the paint not in the incised letters. This gives his pieces a "scrimshaw" effect that is very unique. David describes his work in his book, **Using Fimo, A Basic Handbook**.

An article about stamping on polymer clay, in the July/August 1994 issue of Rubberstampmadness, inspired Rene Atkinson, (A.K.A. "Swizzlestick,") to try using polymer clay. Prior to that time she was an avid rubber-stamper, but she now

101. Polymer clay jewlery by Rene Atkinson.

102. Polymer clay pins by David Edwards.

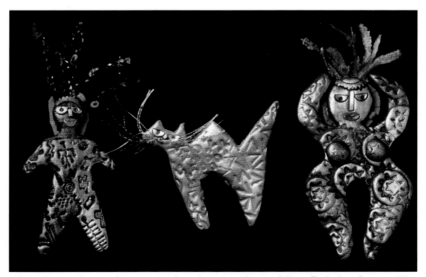

103. Brooches of stamped polymer clay with a finish of metallic powders, by Lynn Sward.

combines techniques and has become a fine polymer clay jewelry designer.

Dawn Graham textures her polymer-clay beads with a great assortment of objects which include cake decorating tips, wire, screws, crumpled papers, sea shells, corks, and old brooches. Such items are hard to use as stamps on paper but are easily pressed into soft, unbaked polymer clay. Dawn coats the unbaked clay with a light dusting of cornstarch or talc, presses the object into the clay and then bakes it with the object still embedded. After the baked piece has cooled, she removes the object, thus creating a mold she can use many times. (The light dusting of cornstarch or talc makes it easier to remove the embedded items from the clay.)

Ileen Shefferman and Barbie Koncher work with natural clay which they stamp and fire in a kiln.

And another world for stamping is opened up to you!

104. Polymer clay beads with impressed marks from found objects. Metallic powders applied before baking, beads are strung with Austrian crystal beads added, by Dawn Graham.

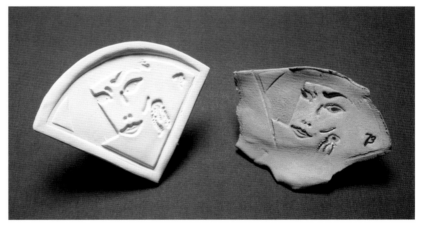

105. Natural pottery clay pins by Barbie Koncher.

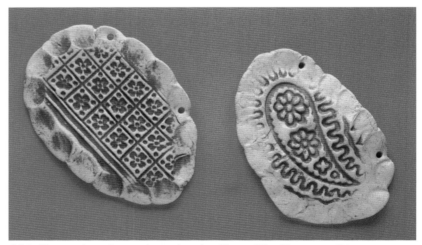

106. Natural pottery clay pins by Ileen Shefferman. Stamps are from fragments of antique wooden wall paper blocks and original carved designs.

107. Stamped fabric with machine stitching by Sara Austin.

Chapter 16:

Stitches And Stamps

 titches with stamping? It may seem to be a strange combination, but it works! With this combination you can create such items as stationery, greeting cards, gift tags, ornaments, and bookmarks, and each item will be unique.

To combine stamping and sewing machine stitching, start with a blank piece of medium weight paper. You need paper sturdy enough to take the sewing, yet not so heavy that the needle cannot pass through it. Use a number 11 sewing machine needle and poly-cotton thread. If you want to use a metallic thread, use it only for the top stitching or for the bottom stitching, but not for both at the same time. That way you'll reduce the chance of thread breakage.

You'll need room to maneuver your project under the sewing machine needle, so keep your stamped design towards the edge of the paper. If you are making a greeting card, open the card flat so you will not sew front and back together. Place the stamped design under the pressure foot and lower the foot onto the paper. Proceed using a straight stitch. Sew around the stamped image, on top of it, or both. A straight stitch, rather than a decorative stitch, produces the best results. Too many stitches in one area, will weaken the paper, make it look "chewed up" and may result in tearing it.

When you have finished the stitching, cut the threads, leaving tails four to five inches long. Raise the pressure foot and remove the piece from the machine carefully, to prevent the tail threads from tearing the paper. If you want both tails on the underside, thread the top tail through a regular needle and gently pull it through to the back. To prevent the stitching from raveling, tie the tails together and clip off the excess thread close to the knot. If you prefer, you can leave both ends on top. For a decorative look, fray them so they feather out, or thread beads or sequins onto them, or add a group of threads to them to make a small tassel.

I've noticed in my own work than the stitching on the back of the card sometimes resembles an object, face, or animal. If you, too, find such images, augment them by painting a dot where you think an eye would go, or by drawing in feathers to clothe a bird, etc.

If you don't want the stitching to show on the underside of your card, cut out a paper backing and glue it to over the stitching you want to conceal. If, on the other hand, you want your stitching to have a definite design on the underside of the card, you must plan your design so that both sides of the card will show the design well.

You might try stamping over your stitching. That way both the stitching and the paper will take on the stamped colors. Because the stitches are on top of the paper, however, you may have to use more pressure when stamping to get good ink coverage on both the stitching and the paper.

Here's a new frontier - stitching combined with stamping. Embroiderers may enjoy this challenge, too.

Abstract Designs

Abstract designs on rubber stamps can be particularly versatile. If you haven't drawn abstract designs before, start by drawing a cloud or by doodling

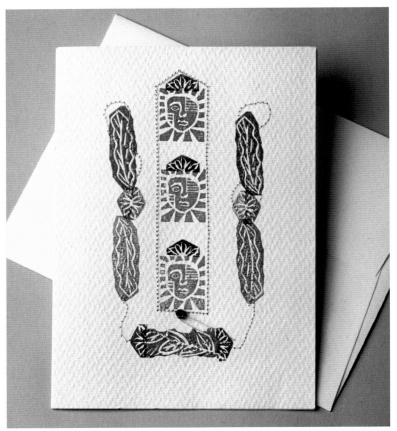

108. Stamped and stitched card by Pat Berlin.

109. Stamped fabric with machine stitching by Sara Austin.

74

on paper. When you have a shape that pleases you, transfer the design onto an eraser and carve it. Since it is an abstract design, it may not have a true top or bottom. To help you keep track of your positioning and stamping sequences when you actually use the stamp, mark the sides of the eraser with a 1, 2, 3, and 4 using permanent ink. If you always do this in a clock-wise direction, your erasers will be consistently marked.

Now take some scrap paper and try out your new stamp! Stamp all four positions and label each one. How would position "1" look next to another position? Try many variations, then do a repeated stamping to create an over-all pattern or border.

You can "butt" the images so they touch each other, or you could leave a small space between them. You can also stagger the images, like brick-work. For special effects, you can stamp a few images before re-inking the stamp and get a "fading-out look," or you may stamp rows of different colors.

You can use repetitive abstract designs in any number of ways, from borders on stationery and envelopes, to designs for book covers or greeting cards.

Now, how do you think your abstract designs would look with some of your other stamps? Try them and see.

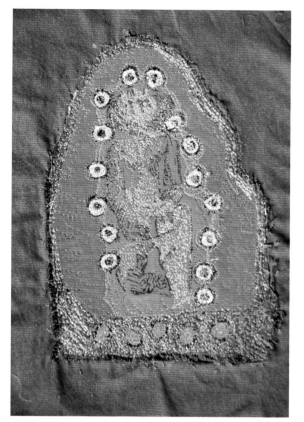

110. Stamped fabric with machine stitching by Sara Austin.

111. Abstract design, from computer printout to finished stamp by Steve Bress.

112. Book art as creative correspondence by Michael Jacobs, photo by Bill Wickett.

Chapter 17:

Handmade Books

o you remember your first handmade book? In kindergarten you may have drawn pictures of your family on construction paper, and presented them to your teacher for binding. That book binding probably consisted of two holes punched at one edge, with a length of bright yarn threaded through them. A bow was tied in the front, and you were published! A private printing, of course, but you were thrilled.

The size of a book and the shape of its pages are as individual as you make them. A handmade book does not necessarily need words to be understood and enjoyed. It may be a book into which you will write later, or it may contain a story line made with stamped designs in a language everyone can understand and appreciate.

Before creating your own library of books, consider the materials you might want to combine with your stamps - interesting paper scraps, cut-out illustrations, old picture post cards, used postage stamps, mail, bits of cloth, and other items that could be used for collage. Survey the materials you have at hand to see what you would like to use. Your first book may be a notebook, a diary or a journal, with just a bit of stamping on the corners of the pages, or the basic book that follows.

A Basic Book

Let's start with the inside pages of a basic book. Gather all your bookmaking materials together - paper, cardboard for the covers, glue, hole punch, a small amount of ribbon or cord for binding, staples, as well as the stamps and stamp pads you think you'll use. Cut your paper and cover material to the size you want your book to be and place the cut pages and your other bookmaking materials before you on a work surface.

Now, design some of the pages of your book using an assortment of the stamping methods you've learned so far. Use one or two similar shades of color for a monochromatic effect, or several colors for a brighter effect. Leave one side of each page blank. Do several sheets in this method and leave room for the text you may wish to add later. Embellish your covers and perhaps add a title.

It's time now to assemble your book. Punch two or three holes at the top or sides of the pages and the covers and thread ribbon, cord, yarn, or leather laces through the holes. Knot or make a bow of the ends, to secure them.

An Accordion-Fold Book

An accordion-fold book is made from one, long, rectangular piece of paper that is folded into sections, and two pieces of cardboard for the front and back covers. For an example of this type of book, we will use one-half of a single sheet of 11" by 17" paper. (In small quantities, 11" by 17" paper can be obtained from a photocopy shop.)

Cut the sheet into two 5-1/2" by 17" pieces. Put one of the sheets aside to be used for a second book. With the 17" dimension running horizontally, cut off 3/4" from one of the narrow ends. Then, with a light pencil line, mark off 3 1/4" sections. These will be your fold lines. In order to make a neat fold, however, each pencil line needs to be indented or scored. To make a slight indentation in the paper without breaking through, use a butter knife, a knitting needle or, if you love tools as I do, a bone folding tool. That tool looks like a round ended letter opener and is available in art supply stores.

After you have designed and completed every page of your book, fold the pages as follows. At the first line, (see diagram 115) fold the paper towards you. At the second line, fold the

113. Hand made and hand stamped book by Ed Hutchins.

114. Inside pages of hand made book by Ed Hutchins.

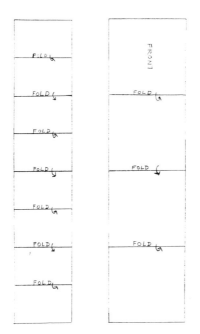

115. Accordian fold book pattern.

paper away from you. Follow this same sequence for the remaining folds.

In order to bind the book properly, the covers should be at least a half-inch wider than the pages. Punch two or three holes at the left side of the covers. Glue the last panel to the inside back cover, bind the covers together, and you have made your first accordion-fold book.

Books of Many Types

"Books can be a sculptural method for storing and sharing information," says book designer Ed Hutchins of Cairo, New York. Ed owns and operates a studio called "Editions" in which he creates hand made books in small editions. To him, books are visual images, with unfolding pages, sequences of ideas, unusual bindings, and molded cases. Ed produces non-traditional books with pop-up pages, origami-like pages which unfold, or pages which become three-dimensional shapes.

Rubber stamping plays an important role in the making of these books, which are predominantly miniatures. Among his many rubber stamps are several alphabet sets, in different sizes, which he uses to print the text of his books, one letter at a

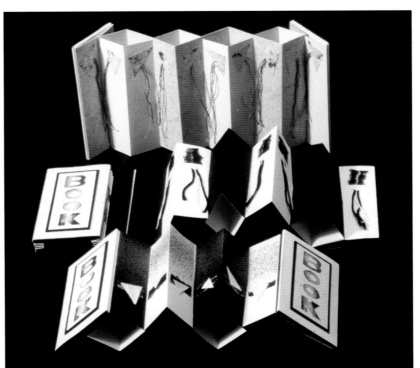

116. Three interlocking accordian fold books, 3" x 6" closed, by Michael Jacobs, photo by Bill Wickett.

117. Stamped, collaged and constructed boxes with pull out drawers, by Michael Jacobs.

time! To produce these books, Ed culls from his amazing collection of scrap paper, paper board, stickers, candy containers, candle molds, dowels, key chains, industrial scraps, and a host of other items from the world of recycled treasures. Some books are produced in a limited-edition series whereas others are strictly one-of-a-kind.

Judy and Michael Jacobs of Seattle, Washington, are also talented book designers. They not only make books, but also boxes of all kinds and interactive sculptures.

Books can be a personal reflection of your inner thoughts, both conscious and unconscious, and without words of explanation. Margo Klass' approach to hand-made books is unique because of the assortment of materials she chooses when creating her one-of-a-kind books. These multi-media books may include rubber stamping, pen-and-ink drawing, a census form, ribbons and threads, paper folding or whatever seems interesting and appropriate to her on that day. The books shown here are but a few of Margo's many creations. She is an accomplished teacher of fine art and has exhibited her work through-

118. Margo Klass' tunnel book.

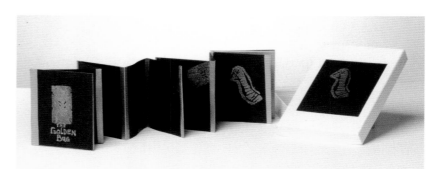

119. Accordian book with embossed stamp, by Pat Berlin.

120. Hand made stamped books, by Pat Berlin.

out the Washington, D.C. area.

Polymer clay, primarily used for the making of jewelry and art objects, has also been used in creative ways to make books. Covers, or entire books, can be made of polymer clay and assembled as described earlier. Rubber stamps and lettering can be pressed into the clay before baking, or stamping and additional items can be applied after the clay has baked and cooled. The holes for binding the book can be put in before the clay is baked, or drilled into the baked clay using a hand drill and a small diameter bit.

Ironic, isn't it, that we have come so far in the last few thousand years, but still enjoy writing on clay tablets!

121. Triangle Books and Portfolios, 4" x 4" closed, by Michael Jacobs, photo by Bill Wickett.

122. "Dulce Rey" a handmade book by Ed Hutchins.

123. Hand made accordian fold book by Margo Klass.

124. Original design, stamped and stitched by Shirley Ende-Saxe on cotton.

Chapter 18:

Quilts, Clothing and Rubber Stamps

Quilts

 any nationally acclaimed quilters combine rubber stamping with quilting to create unique works of art. Stamping allows you to create pictorial images that would be more difficult to accomplish with just fabric, needle and thread.

In order to print properly on fabric, however, your stamps may have to be carved more deeply than those intended for printing on paper. Commercial stamps may print well on fabrics, but try them first on a piece of scrap fabric to make sure.

Instead of your usual stamp pad inks, use fabric paints or fabric dyes for your stamping, since these are permanent and will allow your fabric to be washed or dry-cleaned. The fabric dye or fabric paint can be applied to the stamp with a foam-rubber brush, from a stamp pad saturated with the dye, or from a thin layer of fabric paint spread onto a glass surface.

Natural fabrics, such as cotton or silk, absorb the paint or dye more readily than synthetic fibers. Cotton fabrics should be washed with a mild laundry soap or detergent before being stamped, to remove any sizing or finishing materials added by the mill. Bleached-white or natural silk fabric, specifically sold for batik, painting, or dyeing purposes, should be ready to stamp immediately.

Since different fabric dyes and fabric paints may work differently on different fabrics, (some may be best for cotton but not good for silk, for example), it's best to practice on a scrap before you attempt a big project. For the best possible results, follow the dye manufacturer's recommendations and directions.

Here is a quilt by Jeanne Williamson of Natick, Maine. Jeanne carves erasers in different geometric shapes and patterns, applies fabric paints to the carved blocks, and stamps the fabric to be quilted. She uses 100% cotton, in different textures and weights. After letting the fabric dry completely, she applies another layer of paint on top of the first layer, using different stamps and different colors, repeating this procedure until she gets the effect she wants. For her last step, she heat-sets the paints to the fabric. The quilt illustrated is a small wall quilt.

Danita Rafalovich, of Los Angeles, California, is also an extraordinary quilt maker, who combines intricate quilting with a multitude of rubber stamp designs. Danita's fabric-of-choice is 100% cotton, pre-washed and well ironed. She uses a fabric dye which she applies to her

125. Heart stamped on cotton and quilted by Barbara Bockman.

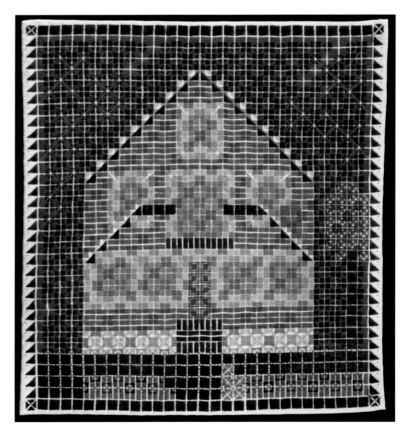

126. Stamped and quilted by Jeanne Williamson.

84

stamps with a one-inch poly-foam brush. The quilt blocks are machine pieced, appliquéd, and quilted. One of the quilts illustrated here is a work she calls "The Chocolate Electric Carrot Happy Birthday Quilt." (Photos 127-128)

Clothing

Hand-stamped clothing with original designs is the heart and soul of "Hot Potatoes," a company started and owned by Mary Benagh O'Neil, of Nashville, Tennessee. When Mary started the company in 1984, she used stamps carved from potatoes. The potatoes were soon replaced by longer lasting and more substantial carved erasers. "Hot Potatoes" produces a kit for printing T-shirts and other clothing. The kit contains stamps, brushes, paints, and instructions, and comes in a replica of the old-fashioned, string, potato bag. (See the Resources section.)

In this world of mass production, it is hard to find neckties as unique as those made by Betty O'Mara and Flora Adams, surface designers who exhibit at the Torpedo Factory Art Center in Alexandria, Virginia. They carve their erasers from original designs, apply fabric dyes or fabric paints to their stamps, and then

127. Front of quilt. Stamped and quilted by Danita Rafalovich.

128. Back of quilt. Stamped and quilted by Danita Rafalovich.

85

print their designs onto silk or cotton tie fabric.

Claire Chytilo, another surface designer, also exhibits her one-of-a-kind apparel pieces at the Torpedo Factory Art Center. Claire carves her own stamps to create unique designs for her fabrics of cotton, silk, and vibrant-colored chiffons. The piece shown here is a reversible vest made of cotton.

Terry Foreman of Newark, Delaware, designs soft jewelry. For her handmade, whimsical works, she applies fabric paints to carved erasers, prints her fabric, then adds a bit of stenciling and decorative stitching to complete her designs. After the surface design is completed, batting and a backing fabric are added, and the three layers are hand stitched together. Beading is sometimes added. Terry carves erasers with her own designs, but she also uses commercial stamps — with copyright permission of course!

129. Stamp set by Hot Potatoes.

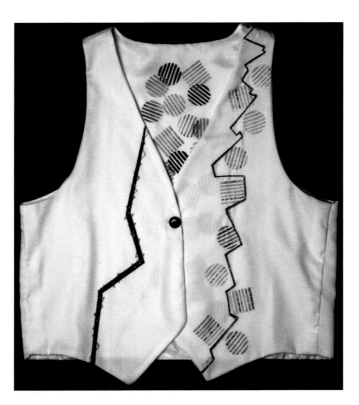

130. Hand stamped vest by Claire Chytilo.

131. Stamped and beaded pin by Terry Foreman.

132. Stamped and stitched pin by Terry Foreman

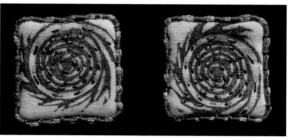

133. Stamped and stitched earrings by Terry Foreman.

134. Hand stamped ties. Left by Betty O'Mara. Right by Flora Adams.

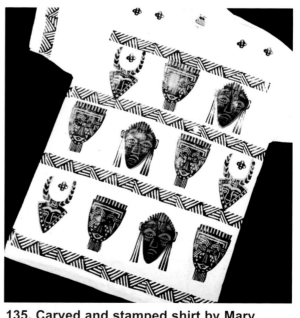

135. Carved and stamped shirt by Mary Benagh O'Neil (Hot Potatoes).

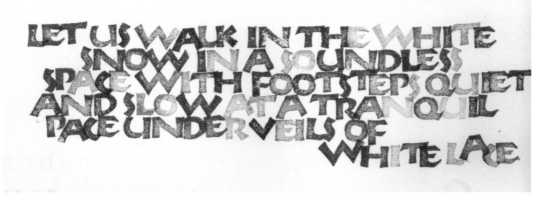

136. By Linda Levine.

137. Hand carved eraser stamping and calligraphy by Linda Levine.

138. Hand carved eraser calligraphy illustrations by Julie Hagan Bloch. Haiku poetry by Daniel Samuel Bloch.

Chapter 19:

Calligraphy

alligraphy, the art of beautiful and elegant handwriting, can enhance your creations even if you are not a calligrapher yourself. There are entire calligraphic alphabets and initials now available on rubber stamps.

Calligraphy can be combined with block letter printing for a dramatic effect. Linda Peterson Levine, calligrapher and designer from Annandale, Virginia has used both methods in the illustration shown here. The poem was printed first, using her own hand carved letters, and the calligraphy was then applied over the printing.

Julie Hagan Bloch of Hurleyville, New York, an extraordinarily talented person, designs the Haiku books written by her husband, David Bloch. She uses hand carved letters and illustrations. Faux postage stamps are also a carving favorite for this talented artist and several will adorn an envelope along with traditional postage. Julie's wise advice on patience is shown on a hand carved stamp (right) and is a most remarkable achievement.

139. By Julie Hagan Bloch.

An enduring, all purpose stamp is the one Pat Conner, of Falls Church, Virginia, carved from an eraser (right). A simple "Thank You" stamp could have been purchased ready made, but Pat liked the challenge of carving one in her own calligraphic style. Her original artwork was done on vellum graph paper which was printed with blue ink. The blue ink disappeared when the paper went through the copier, leaving only her artwork, which she then transferred to an eraser for carving. (See Chapter 10.)

140. By Pat Conners.

ARTISTS

Amt, Kathleen
4011 30th St.
Mt. Ranier, MD 20712
Plates # 47, 82

Atkinson, R.M.
("Swizzlestick")
5013 Dalton Road
Chevy Chase, MD 20815
Plate # 101

Austin, Sara
3301 Via La Selva
Palos Verdes, CA 90274
Plates # 107, 109, 110

Benagh, Mary O'Neil
"Hot Potatoes"
2109 Grantland Ave.
Nashville, TN 37204
Plates # 35, 129, 135

Berlin, Pat
2540 Inlynnview Road
Virginia Beach, VA 23454
Plates # 1, 10, 11, 14, 15,
16, 17, 18, 19, 20, 23, 24,
25, 26, 27, 30, 32, 33, 34,
40, 41, 42, 43, 45, 46, 48,
51, 53, 54, 59, 60, 64, 66,
67, 68, 69, 70, 73, 74, 76,
77, 80, 83, 85, 86, 87, 88,
89, 92, 93, 94, 97, 98, 108,
119, 120

Bloch, Julie Hagan
51 Mongaup Road
Hurleyville, NY 12747
Plate # 138

Brand, R.R.
"NAGA"
25 Merehai Place
Snell's Beach, Warkworth
1240, New Zealand
Plates # 28, 31

Bockman, Barbara S.
3607 Glenbrook Rd.
Fairfax, VA 22031
Plate # 125

Brooks, Jamie
2503 Brighton Ct.
Vienna, VA 22180
Plates # 21, 49

Chytilo, Claire
7427 Rebecca Dr.
Alexandria, VA 22307
Plate # 130

Conner, Pat
2312 Brilyn Place
Falls Church, VA 22046
Plate # 140

Edwards, David
USCD 200 Arbor Dr.
San Diego, CA 92103
Plate # 102

Foreman, Terry
"Design in Mind"
307 Mason Dr.
Newark, DE 19711
Plates # 96, 131, 132, 133

Graham, Dawn
936 N. Chestnut
Arlington Heights, IL
60004
Plate # 104

Hutchins, Ed
"Editions"
PO Box 895
Cairo, NY 12413
Plates # 113, 114, 122

Jacobs, Judy
PO Box 19458
Seattle, WA 98109
Plates # 50, 65, 81

Jacobs, Michael
PO Box 19458
Seattle, WA 98109
Plates # 84, 112, 116, 117,
121

Johnson, Nancy
6902 Constance Drive
Springfield, VA 22150
Plate # 99

Klass, Margo
6310 Poe Rd.
Bethesda, MD 20817
Plates # 118, 123

Koncher, Barbie
1110 Saint Andrew Dr.
Discovery Bay, CA 94514
Plate # 105

Levine, Linda P.
8710 Braeburn Dr.
Annandale, VA 22003
Plates # 136, 137

O'Mara, Betty
1202 Kelly St. SW
Vienna, VA 22180
Plate # 134

Rafalovich, Danita
3956 Minerva Ave.
Los Angeles, CA 90066
Plates # 127, 128

Saxe, Shirley Ende
"Rubber Grace"
2306 New Haven Ave.
Cuyahoga Falls, OH 44223
Plate # 124

Shefferman, Ileen
6460 Madison Ct.
McLean, VA 22101
Plate # 106

Sward, Lynne
625 Bishop Dr.
Virginia Beach, VA 23455
Plate # 103

Thomas, Larry
2006 McLendon Ave.
Atlanta, GA 30307
Plate # 78

Williamson, Jeanne
18 Erlandson Road
Natick, MA 01760
Plate # 126

ART SUPPLIES

Color Box tm
Clearsnap, Inc.
PO Box 98
Anacortes, WA

Deka Permanent Fabric
Paint
Decart, Inc.
LaMoille Industrial Park
Box 309
Morrisville, VT 05661

Hunt Manufacturing Co.
230 South Broad Street
Philadelphia, PA 19102

Kaleidacolor tm
Tsukineko, Inc.
15411 NE 95th St.
Redmond, WA 98052

Color It tm
Ranger Industries
15 Park Rd.
Tinton Falls, NJ 07724

Daniel Smith, Inc.
4150 First Ave. South
Seattle, WA 98124

PAPER COMPANIES

Paper Access, Inc.
23 West 18th St.
New York, NY 10011

Paper Direct
205 Chubb Ave.
Lyndhurst, NJ 07071

Paper Source
232 West Chicago Ave.
Chicago, IL 60610

Premier Papers, Inc
PO Box 845
Mankato, MN 56002

PERIODICALS

Eraser Carvers Quarterly
Mick Matther
PO Box 222
Clay, NY 13040

Letter Arts Review
1624 24 Ave. SW
Norman, OK 73027

Page Two, Inc.
PO Box 77167
Washington, DC 20013

RUBBERSTAMPMADNESS
408 SW Monroe, #210
Corvallis, OR 97330

Somerset Studio
Stampington & Co.
22992 Mill Creek
Laguna Hills, CA 92653

Vamp Stamp News
PO Box 386
Hanover, MD 21076

RUBBER STAMP
COMPANIES

Binney & Smith, Inc.
1100 Church Lane
P.O. Box 431
Easton, PA 18044

CRAF-T Products
P.O. Box 83
Fairmont, MN 56031

Good Stamps
30901 Timberline Rd.
Willits, CA 95490

Hot Potatoes
209 10 Ave. S. Suite 311
Nashville, TN 37203

Ivory Coast
17725 NE 65 St., #240
Redmond, WA 98025

Mars Tokyo
PO Box 65006
Baltimore, MD 21209

Marvy/Uchida of America
3535 Del Amo Blvd.
Torrance, CA 90503

Meer Images
P.O. Box 12
Arcata, CA 95518

OM Studio
P.O. Box 448
Seaside, OR 97138

The Paper Cat
218 First Ave. S.
Seattle, WA 98104

Paper Source
232 W. Chicago Ave.
Chicago, IL 60610

Personal Stamp Exchange
360 Sutton Place
Santa Rosa, CA 95407

Rubber Poet
PO Box 218
Rockville, UT 84763

Staedtler, Inc.
21900 Plummer St.
Chatsworth, CA 91311